Springer Series: FOCUS ON WOMEN

Violet Franks, Ph.D., Series Editor

Confronting the major psychological, medical, and social issues of today and tomorrow, *Focus on Women* provides a wide range of books on the changing concerns of women.

VOLUME 1

THE SAFETY OF FERTILITY CONTROL
Editor-in-Chief: Louis G. Keith, M.D.
Associate Editors: Deryck R. Kent, M.D., Gary S. Berger, M
and Janelle R. Brittain, M.B.A.

VOLUME 2

THERAPY WITH WOMEN: A Feminist Philosophy of Treatment
Susan Sturdivant, Ph.D.

VOLUME 3

SHELTERING BATTERED WOMEN
A National Study and Service Guide
Albert R. Roberts, D.S.W.

VOLUME 4

WOMEN OVER FORTY: Visions and Realities
Marilyn R. Block, Ph.D., Janice L. Davidson, M.S., and Jean D. Grambs, Ed.D.

VOLUME 5

THE STEREOTYPING OF WOMEN
Its Effects on Mental Health
Violet Franks, Ph.D. and Esther D. Rothblum, Ph.D.

VOLUME 6

THE BATTERED WOMAN SYNDROME
Lenore E. Walker, Ed.D.

VOLUME 7

WOMEN THERAPISTS WORKING WITH WOMEN
New Theory and Process of Feminist Therapy
Claire M. Brody, Ph.D., Editor

VOLUME 8

CAREER GUIDE FOR WOMEN SCHOLARS
Suzanna Rose, Ph.D.

Suzanna Rose, Ph.D., currently holds a joint appointment in psychology and Women's Studies at the University of Missouri-St. Louis. She received her Ph.D. from the University of Pittsburgh where she was part of a core of feminist scholars. There she began studying how friendships and professional networks affect the quality of women's (and men's) lives and work experience. Both her research and her experience as a faculty member made her aware of the need for women to develop specific career strategies to overcome the problems they confront. With the encouragement of Irene Frieze, a mentor and then-President of The Psychology of Women Division (Division 35) of the American Psychological Association, she set out to publish these strategies so other women scholars could benefit from them.

Career Guide
for Women Scholars

Suzanna Rose, Ph.D.

Editor

Prepared under the auspices of
The Psychology of Women Division
of the American Psychological Association
(Division 35)

SPRINGER PUBLISHING COMPANY
New York

Springer Publishing Company, Inc.
536 Broadway
New York, NY 10012

86 87 88 89 90 / 5 4 3 2 1

Library of Congress Cataloging-in-Publication Data

Career guide for women scholars.

   (Springer series, focus on women ; v. 8)
   "A product of the Psychology of Women Division
(Division 35) of the American Psychological Association."
   Bibliography: p.
   Includes index.
   1. Women college graduates—Employment—United States.
2. Job hunting—United States. 3. Vocational guidance
for women—United States. I. Rose, Suzanna.
II. American Psychological Association. Division of
the Psychology of Women. III. Series.
HD6053.U5C37 1986   650.1′4′024042   86-6532
ISBN 0-8261-5411-5 (pbk.)

Printed in the United States of America

Contents

■ One: The Academic Career Path

Contributors

Rosalie J. Ackerman, Ph.D., is a neuropsychologist at the Rehabilitation Hospital for Special Services in State College, Pennsylvania. Formerly she was Clinical Assistant Professor at the University of North Carolina at Chapel Hill, where she taught courses on adult development and aging, biological psychology, personality, and microcomputer applications. She received degrees in biochemistry and psychology from Iowa State University. An experienced career-changer, she has numerous publications representing her work in both disciplines. Her current research interests include the neuropsychology of adult development, psychiatric disorders, and developmental/aging diseases. She currently is exploring how microcomputers can be used in neuro- and cognitive rehabilitation. In terms of women's issues, her research areas include stress management, career-changing strategies of middle-aged women, and group and family psychotherapy.

Martha E. Banks, Ph.D., is a graduate of Brown University and the University of Rhode Island. Her graduate work was in clinical psychology with a specialization in family psychotherapy. She is employed at the Brecksville Veterans Administration Medical Center where, as clinical geropsychologist, she works with long-term medical and rehabilitation patients. In addition, she does neurological retraining and develops software for this purpose and has offered continuing education workshops on the applications of microcomputers to psychology. She has taught geriatric ethics, family psychotherapy with the elderly, and neuropsychology. Her research interests include the status of Black women in psychology, computerized cognitive rehabilitation for geriatric patients, and the psychological applications of music.

Denise R. Barnes, Ph.D., is an Assistant Professor in the Department of Psychology at the University of North Carolina at Chapel Hill. She received her masters and doctoral degrees from the Institute of Advanced Psychological Studies at Adelphi University. Her postdoctoral work was completed at the Center for the Study of Aging and Human Development at Duke University Medical School. Her present scholarly interests are cross-cultural psychology and adult development and aging. She is particularly interested in clinical interventions for aging populations and cross-generational coping strategies.

Phyllis Bronstein received her Ph.D. in social psychology in 1979 from Harvard University. She held a clinical postdoctoral fellowship in Ethnicity and Mental Health at Harvard University Medical School and Brandeis University, and taught for a year at Wellesley College. She is currently on the faculty of the clinical psychology program at the University of Vermont, where she teaches family therapy, group dynamics and group therapy, and personality. Her research has been in the areas of family relations and children's and adolescents' socioemotional development, small group interaction, and women's professional advancement in psychology. She is in the process of editing a book on fatherhood and another on gender and minority issues in the teaching of psychology. She has accomplished the above while also being the primary parent for her three children, and marvels at the fact that she has survived "having it all."

Linda Garnets received her doctorate in clinical psychology from the University of Michigan in 1978. She is a psychotherapist and organizational consultant in private practice in Los Angeles. Her professional activities include being President-Elect of the Los Angeles Society of Clinical Psychologists, Chair of the Committee on the Status of Women for the American Society on Aging, Regional Coordinator of the Association for Women in Psychology, and Chair of the Continuing Education Task Force of Division 35 (The Psychology of Women) of the American Psychological Association. In addition, she has trained clinical psychologists new to the field.

Judith L. Gibbons received her doctorate from Carnegie-Mellon University in 1976. She did two postdoctorates in neuroscience, one at Albert Einstein College of Medicine, the other at Columbia University College of Physicians and Surgeons. In 1979 she joined the psychology department at St. Louis University as an assistant professor. In her first bid for tenure, she was denied tenure at the level of the University president, in part because of a new policy which prohibited tenuring the last member of any department. The subsequent year she was awarded tenure and promoted to associate professor.

Susan Gore, Ph.D., is a consultant in the San Francisco Bay area specializing in nonprofit organizational development, conference planning, and public speaking. She is coordinator of the Association for Women in Psychology and secretary for the Association of Lesbian and Gay Psychologists, past director of the National Women's Studies Association, and a former academic with five years of university experience in the U.S. and Western Europe.

Laurie Larwood obtained her Ph.D. in psychology from Tulane University in 1974 with a social-developmental dissertation. Her first position was with the School of Management at SUNY — Binghamton teaching organizational behavior. Next, she taught industrial-organizational psychology at the Claremont Colleges, where she chaired the Claremont McKenna College Psychology Department. She is now Head of the Department of Management at the University of Illinois at Chicago's College of Business Administration. Prior to entering academics, Laurie was one of the founders and President of Davis Instruments Corporation in California. She has written extensively on women in management, and her books include *Women in Management* and *Women's Career Development* (forthcoming). She is an editor of *Women and Work: An Annual Review* and *Journal of Management Case Studies*, and has served on several editorial boards. As well, she has chaired the Academy of Management's Women in Management Division and is currently conference chair for the R&D/Technology/Innovation Division and the Women and Organizations International Conference. Laurie has served as an expert witness on cases involving equal employment opportunity and motivation.

Kathryn Quina earned an uneventful Ph.D. in experimental psychology (perceptual development) at the University of Georgia in 1973. The intervening years in academia were largely spent learning from her mistakes, personal and professional. Her present position as an associate professor at the University of Rhode Island includes administrative responsibilities for the psychology program for adult (mostly women) students at the URI College of Continuing Education, and for special summer programming. As a Lilly Postdoctoral Teaching Fellow (1979–1980) she examined her role as a professor; this year she will work for gender balance in methodology courses as a National Mellon Scholar at the Wellesley Center for Research on Women. She is currently working on a book for counselors of sexual assault and harassment victims. Among her rewarding service activities are work with the American Psychological Association's Division 35 (Psychology of Women) on task forces in continuing education and teaching the psychology of women, and in local women's groups.

Linda Rogers is a graduate student in the clinical psychology program at the University of Missouri-St. Louis, where she is in the dissertation phase of graduate study. Linda's professional interests include women's career-home conflicts, the study of sex roles, and women's adult development. Clinically, she is interested primarily in ego psychology and the treatment of borderline and narcissistic personality disorders. The mother of four teenage children, Linda returned to graduate school as an "older" student and is hoping to complete the Ph.D. and move on to a professional role before her children do.

Joanna Bunker Rohrbaugh is in private practice in Boston and on the faculty of the Departments of Psychiatry at Harvard Medical School and Massachusetts General Hospital. In addition to supervising the clinical work of postdoctoral psychology interns, Joanna teaches at Harvard a variety of courses on the Psychology of Women. She is the author of *Women: Psychology's Puzzle.*

Sharon Toffey Shepela is a Professor of Psychology and Director of the Women's Research Institute, and Director of Research at The Counseling Center of Hartford College for Women. She received her B.A. and M.S. from The Pennsylvania State University and her Ph.D. in Experimental Psychology from Cornell University. She has conducted workshops on career advice for women psychologists for several years. With her dual appointment she considers herself to be inside academe, outside the mainstream.

Jayne E. Stake is currently Professor of Psychology and Clinical Director at the University of Missouri-St. Louis. Her awareness as a graduate student of how seldom women were encouraged to pursue graduate training led to her interest in women's achievement and career aspirations. Since receiving her Ph.D. from Arizona State University, she has investigated many topics related to women's career confidence and motivation, including the effects of leadership and assertiveness training, role models, and feedback on women's and men's achievement. Jayne also is a Consulting Editor for the *Psychology of Women Quarterly*. Her interest in encouraging female achievement extends to her two daughters, Soni and Karin.

Janice D. Yoder completed her doctorate in social psychology in 1979 at the State University of New York at Buffalo. Her first job was as a visiting assistant professor in the psychology department at Washington University, a tenuous position that was ripe for her first introduction to severe sexual harassment. Her next position, as one of the first two women to be civilian Distinguished Visiting Professors at the U.S. Military Academy at West Point, gave her firsthand experiences as a token woman, as well as the opportunity to study the process of tokenism for the newly matriculated women cadets. After a semester at the academy, she left West Point to return to St. Louis, where she joined her fiance and the faculty of Webster University. Both her marriage and her position at Webster, a small private university with many nontraditional-age students, where women comprise half the faculty at all academic levels, are just the right fit.

Preface

Career Guide for Women Scholars is a product of the Task Force on Strategies for Getting and Keeping a Job. The task force was established in 1983 by Irene Hanson Frieze, president of Division 35 (Psychology of Women) of the American Psychological Association. The purpose of Division 35 is to promote the research and study of women and to encourage the integration of information about women into psychology and society.

The objective of the task force was to develop guidelines and advice that would be useful to recently graduated women Ph.D.s. This book is the culmination of our two years of effort. We have endeavored to present solutions and alternatives that would enhance women's self respect and value both as professionals and as women. We hope you benefit from our experience and our efforts.

Acknowledgments

Many women assisted in the development of this project. I would like to thank Irene Frieze for conceiving of the task force that led to this product, and for her support in publishing it. Gratitude is extended to Victoria Sork for her encouragement, editorial assistance, and generosity, particularly during the final stages. Susan Hartmann's help and advice also are gratefully acknowledged. Special thanks are extended to the contributors, who made editing this volume such a pleasurable task.

In addition, the assistance of the following reviewers and supporters was greatly appreciated: Shelley Canter, Eleanor Hall, Phyllis Katz, Nancy Russo, Barbara Wallston, Maria Vegega.

Introduction

The aim in assembling this book was to focus on nontraditional advice that would help women graduate students and recent Ph.D.s as they begin their careers. Contributors were asked to reflect on advice in the category of "what I wish I'd known then," and to pass their ideas on to other women. The intent was to go beyond traditional advice, such as how to dress for success or how to learn academic gamesmanship. Instead, we gleaned from our experiences strategies that enabled us to survive and sometimes flourish in spite of the structure of the profession, discrimination, and academic unemployment.

In the first section, "The Academic Career Path," the focus is on strategies for earning tenure. The chapter by Phyllis Bronstein on "Applying for Academic Jobs: Strategies for Success" tells recent graduates how to prepare for the job search, format their curriculum vitae, and plan and negotiate the interview. Once the tenure-track position is obtained, the next concern for women is whether or not they are entering the "five-year revolving door." Judith Gibbons in "Pitfalls on the Way to Tenure" and Kathryn Quina in "Helping Yourself to Tenure" address the barriers women confront during the tenure process and propose solutions. Specific strategies to aid in the tenure competition are networking and publishing. These are described in the articles by Suzanna Rose and Jayne Stake, respectively. For black women, academic survival poses even more problems. Denise Barnes identifies these and offers coping strategies in "Transitions and Stresses for Black Women Scholars."

"Individual Issues and Solutions" is the theme of the second section. Advice ranges from narrow to broad. Janice Yoder and Kathryn Quina, in separate chapters, emphasize the obstacles and decisions women are likely to face in their first academic job. Suggestions for graduate students or would-be graduate students are offered in the chapters "The Graduate School Experience," by Linda Rogers and "Middle-aged Women in Job Transition," by Rosalie Ackerman. Black women Ph.D.s outside academe confront some different job issues. Martha Banks gives tips to black women who are trying to survive as professionals in mental health settings. Lesbians constitute an often neglected professional population. In the article "Issues Confronting Lesbian Scholars," Joanna Bunker Rohrbaugh identifies issues and strategies unique to lesbians.

The third section, "Alternatives to Academe," is aimed at women who want to leave academe or who do not get tenure. For women in the mental health professions, one option is to open a private practice. Linda Garnets provides guidelines for women beginning the private practice of psychotherapy. For women who have difficulty thinking about alternatives to academic jobs, Sharon Toffey Shepela provides encouragement and concrete suggestions in "Changing Career Directions: Life Outside the Academic Mainstream." A personal account of academic unemployment and subsequent exciting career changes is recounted by Susan Gore. Last, Laurie Larwood's article on "Career Options and Strategies in Business and Management" provides ideas for a wealth of jobs former scholars can pursue for stimulation and profit.

To enable readers to follow some of our suggestions, organizational contacts and other resources are included in the Appendixes.

Suzanna Rose, Ph.D.

■ one
THE ACADEMIC CAREER PATH

■ 1
Applying for Academic Jobs: Strategies for Success

PHYLLIS BRONSTEIN

The information I will be sharing in this chapter comes from my own experiences during several years on the academic job market. Starting before I graduated, and continuing through a post- doctoral year and another year with a temporary teaching appointment, I was looking for a tenure-track position that would be the right job for me. It was a time-consuming and often frustrating and discouraging process. However, I found that applying for academic jobs is an acquired skill, which I developed as I went along — and I also used those years to expand and develop my qualifications. Two important things I learned were that what may seem like setbacks along the way can turn out to be advantages, and that strokes of luck can come along just when desperation is setting in. Based on the knowlege I gained during those years (and afterwards as a faculty member participating in the hiring of six junior-level people), this chapter will describe a systematic approach toward getting an academic job, focusing on both the preparation and application process.[1] Because it is never too early to start planning for this eventual

---

[1]I first began thinking about these issues and ideas in graduate school, after hearing a talk on getting academic jobs given by two fellow students who had been especially successful at the process. I am grateful to Martha Cox and Rita Coleman for their suggestions, some of which are included here, and which helped me on my way.

career move, I have directed the discussion toward women who are still in graduate school. However, I hope it will also prove useful to women who have their degree, but have not yet found the job of their choice.

THE PREPARATION PHASE

Setting Obtainable Goals

The first and most basic step in the job application process is to decide what you want, and then to go after it. I operate according to the principle that *anything* is achievable, if I (or you, or anyone else) can get sufficient information to figure out how to do it, and put forth enough effort. Of course, this assumes having goals that are at least theoretically obtainable. It *is* possible to get a tenure-track academic position in which you will be able to do the work you want to do. However, given the general scarcity of academic jobs, it may *not* be possible to get such a position if, for example, you are committed to staying in a particular geographic area. You may have to decide between what turn out to be conflicting goals — the kind of job you want versus the location you want — and to redefine your goal so that it is obtainable, taking that conflict into account.

Then expect the goal attainment to take up to four years. Some new Ph.D.s are lucky and find just the job they want during their last year in graduate school, even before they have their degree in hand. Many others, however, spend their years after graduation in postdocs, soft-money research positions, or visiting academic appointments, filling in for regular faculty on sabbatical. These positions should not be regarded as setbacks or signs of not quite having made it onto the academic ladder. Rather, they should be regarded as valuable means of establishing and enhancing your credentials, of making contacts, and of buying time to do a careful and thorough job search, which wasn't possible when you were scrambling to get your dissertation finished. In addition, since there are three times as many jobs available over a three-year period than over a one-year period, it is all the more possible that the right job opportunities will eventually appear — just the kind you have been hoping for, that are looking for someone exactly like you.

Preparing Your Credentials

Obviously it is never too early to start acquiring credentials that will look impressive on your *curriculum vitae* (or "vita," as it is commonly called). Many graduate students, however, are so overwhelmed by the demands of their program that they don't begin thinking about the necessity of acquiring academic credentials until their final year. There are four main areas to consider.

Research and Scholarship.   It is important to present and publish your work as soon as is feasible. If you have been fortunate enough to have assisted or collaborated in a faculty member's research, the process may occur with little extra effort on your part, since most faculty members know how to get their work published, or accepted for conference presentation. On the other hand, you may be one of those who worked alone or in collaboration with another graduate student, because faculty members were either unavailable[2] or doing work that didn't interest you. In these latter instances, the prospect of trying to present or publish your work may seem intimidating at first, since no one has shown you how to go about it. However, you may ultimately find yourself in a stronger position on the job market. Whatever you produce will be your own — and departments look for junior faculty who show the ability to start up and develop their own research programs.

If you haven't yet published your work, you may be doubting that you have anything substantial enough to submit. Chances are that at least some of the work you have done in graduate school is publishable, whether it is an experimental study done for a research practicuum, a review of an area's research literature, or the findings from your dissertation. It is often just a matter of the right format and the right outlet. Your first efforts don't have to appear in the most prestigious journals in your field; there are specialized journals, lesser-known journals, and journals in related fields that are receptive to interesting work that may not fit the rigid (and often arbitrary) criteria of the most prestigious ones. (See Stake chapter for other suggestions.)

---

[2]A number of researchers have presented evidence that faculty tend to take women graduate students less seriously than they do men, and that they are less supportive of women graduate students' career plans (Brodsky, 1974; Freeman, 1972; Holstrom & Holstrom, 1974; Lewis, 1975; Sells, 1973).

Presentations at conferences are much more easily accomplished, and they also indicate that you have undertaken and completed a project which has been deemed worthwhile by your peers. If it is research results you will be presenting, you do not need to have obtained them by the time you submit a paper proposal. You can describe the research process, the analyses that are underway, and the results you expect. It is easier to get proposals accepted for regional conferences, which are often fairly small — and small conferences are much less intimidating for the first-time presenter. Or consider giving a poster session, or if you are feeling very ambitious, organizing and submitting a proposal for a symposium or panel. Having done all the work to prepare the paper, you can usually, with very little additional effort, expand it into an article to submit for publication.

Teaching Experience. When applying for an academic teaching position, it is always advantageous to be able to include college teaching experience as one of your credentials. You can get such experience during graduate school by being a teaching assistant or by teaching a course or two in the continuing education program of your institution or at a local community college. You should make sure to get formal evaluations of your teaching from the students at the end of the course, because if they are positive, you can include them in summary form with your application credentials. If some of the students tell you the course was great, ask them if they would be willing to put their opinions on paper, in the form of a letter to your program chair, with a copy for your own files. This will enable your chair to discuss your teaching ability in specific and glowing terms when she or he writes a letter of recommendation for you. And if you have a number of such letters, they can look very impressive as part of your application credentials.

Additional Work Experience. Work experience beyond assistantships within your department, if it is relevant to the position you will ultimately be seeking, is extremely valuable. In addition, such experience can broaden the range of jobs for which you would be considered. For example, several students in my social psychology graduate program, who did some work with organizational consulting firms, were later offered positions in top-ranking graduate programs in organizational behavior. I did a clinical internship, which made me eligible for some positions in clinical as well as social psychology. And a student I knew in sociology, because of the training and experience he received while working as a computer consultant for the university, became a very viable candidate for departments seeking a methodologist/statistician. You can also enhance your credentials by doing a year or more of postdoctoral training or research. This can be in the form of a fellowship, an internship, or a research or clinical appointment. Ideally, the position should provide you with the opportunity to develop your expertise in a particular area and make additional contacts who will help you in the job-seeking process, as well as with time to increase your scholarly output and publish your work. If the appointment is at a prestigious institution, or affiliated with a well-known person in the field, all the better.

Membership in Professional Organizations.   This is less important than the preceding three areas, but it does make you look more like an up-and-coming professional if you have joined some professional organizations while still in graduate school. In addition, particular organizations may strike a positive chord with a member of a department's job search committee. For example, indication that you belong to the feminist Association for Women in Psychology would endear you to any feminist who happened to be on a psychology search committee. Further, professional organizations provide wonderful opportunities for networking. (See chapter by Rose.)

Lining Up Letters of Recommendation

Unfortunately, it is no longer enough to have *good* letters of recommendation, which verify that you are a bright, hardworking graduate student who has done well in her coursework, has shown initiative in her independent scholarship, and is generally pleasant to have around. The letters, in order to be competitive in a difficult market, have to be filled with *superlatives.* Candidates generally ask only those referees whom they feel will write totally positive things, and most referees tend to oblige, not only saying totally positive things, but overstating them in the process. However, it can also happen that one of your referees, out of misplaced modesty or jealousy, *under*states your excellent qualities, or slips in little remarks about your limitations — and this will have a chilling if not lethal effect on your candidacy every place you apply. This possibility makes selecting your referees a tricky procedure, in which you may end up omitting some professors you have worked with closely because you know they write half-page, understated letters, while cultivating relationships with others whom you haven't worked with at all because you know they write eloquent four-page documents attesting to a candidate's godliness.

Except for some individual misogynist instances, referees seem to be writing letters of recommendation for women that are as positive as those written for men. Earlier studies (Guillemin, Holmstrom, & Garvin, 1979; Hoffman, 1972; Lewis, 1975; Lunneborg & Lillie, 1973) had found that women were praised significantly less than men in a number of important areas, and that appearance, family status, and other irrelevant facts were more frequently included in letters about women. However, recent research of mine (Bronstein, Black, Pfennig, & White, 1986a, 1986b), which analyzed the vitas and letters of applicants for academic jobs in psychology, found that women in fact were praised slightly *more* highly then men in a number of areas, especially by female referees. On the other hand, in one of our studies, referees more often mentioned women's family status — and when they did, they presented it as a burden, whereas when it was mentioned about men, it was generally portrayed as an asset.

Taking all of the above information into account, I believe it is important for women applicants for academic jobs to monitor their letters of recommendation. I trusted to the goodwill and know-how of my referees the first two years I was on the job market — with the following unfortunate results, which I did not discover until much later. One referee said I was a stimulating person, and my data were interesting — period. The rest of the letter was filled with misinformation that underplayed my accomplishments. Another indicated in each letter sent out that I had requested different letters for clinical and nonclinical positions, and then specified which version he was sending. Another, whom I later discovered didn't send out any of the requested letters for four months, began his letter with "As an older woman with children returning to school. . . . " I was invited for a few interviews in those first two years, but I also got some funny responses from departments that were showing hesitant interest in me — which alerted me to the fact that something was amiss. For example, one search committee chair referred to me as a "closet clinician," while another spoke generally about psychology graduates who couldn't get jobs in their own areas, and were trying to pass themselves off as clinicians. Another told me they were looking for a junior-level person, and I had been out a long time, hadn't I? In fact, I had received my Ph.D. a year before; what he really meant (and was misremembering) was that he knew from one of my letters that I was older than the usual junior-level applicant. I should mention here that my vita did not reveal the information they referred to, nor did I at the time look appreciably older than my cohort — which indicated to me that their impressions had in fact been derived from my letters. Similarly, in the study mentioned above, *not one* female applicant indicated on her vita that she had a spouse or children (as opposed to 37 % of the male applicants who did indicate it) — yet 25 % of the letters recommending those female applicants spoke directly about their husband or children.

In addition to perhaps receiving fewer interviews, if you don't take precautions to monitor your letters, you may have the unpleasant experience of inadvertently learning of a negative evaluation. One woman, while retrieving a manuscript from the department job box, came across an alarmingly poor recommendation a faculty member had written for her. Another learned of a damaging letter only because a secretary left it where she, the student, was likely to see it.

There are a number of different ways to monitor your letters. The most straightforward is to try to play some part in the actual letter-writing process. When first asking for a letter, give your referee your vita and any other information that might be helpful (such as a statement of your research interests), plus any information about what you might want or not want emphasized or included for any particular job. Then ask if you might have a copy of the letter for your files. If you are comfortable asking to review it before it is sent out, fine; if not, make sure you have that first unseen version sent to a place you are not really interested in. Once you have seen the letter, you may be able to tactfully negotiate changes. If that fails, and the letter seems unhelpful in its present form, then you at least know not to request any further letters from that referee.

A more indirect approach is to ask the referee to put a copy in your department file which, in fact, you legally have access to. Another method, which can also prove useful if your referees are unreliable about sending letters out promptly, is to ask them to send a copy to a credentials file that you set up in your university's placement office. Here, you have two options: you can retain your legal right to have access to those letters, or you can waive that right.

Many people will advise you to waive your right, claiming that the letters will have more credibility to the recipients if they know referees' confidentiality was protected. There is a small amount of data, based on very limited samples, suggesting that people may give less positive recommendations for graduate school applicants when they know the applicants will not have access to them (Ceci & Peters, 1984), and that graduate school applicants may be more likely to be granted acceptance if their letters were confidential (Schaffer & Tomarelli, 1981). However, my personal experience on both graduate admissions and faculty search committees has been that *no one notices* whether or not applicants have waived their rights. I personally think it is unethical to pressure people, through fear tactics, into waiving their rights, and for this reason, I always urge students not to waive them.

Finally, in choosing your referees, the most important factor is not the person's prestige. It is preferable by far to have an excellent letter from an M.A. level clinical supervisor, whom you had lunch with twice a week and who is your friend and ally, than from a world-famous professor who is notoriously nonsupportive of women, or who only knows you well enough to say that you got an *A* in her or his course. Cultivate relationships with faculty who are known to go to bat for students — ones who will make a few phone calls in your behalf, or will plug you in to their "old boy" or "old girl" network, as well as write a long, eloquent letter extolling your qualifications. It doesn't have to be the ones with whom you do research. You can take courses with the more supportive faculty members and develop an intellectual exchange outside of class. You can keep them informed of your scholarly work and ask their opinions and advice. When the time comes for you to be applying for jobs, they are likely to be very willing to help. And keep in mind that our research (Bronstein et al., 1986a, 1986b) suggests that women tend to be the most supportive referees for women applicants.

Establishing Contacts and Building Networks

We are now seeing not only a growing number of women in academia, but also a substantial number who are dedicated to giving other women a helping hand onto the academic career ladder. Others, who may be less overtly available for support, are supportive of affirmative action policies and wish to see more women hired. There are also some men who fall into the above categories, and plenty of women and men faculty who are simply looking for promising junior colleagues to enhance their department. It is never too early to start making contacts and building networks with people such as these, who can help you in making that first major career step. (See Rose's chapter for further suggestions.)

THE APPLICATION PROCESS

The application process, which is the key phase of the whole job-getting endeavor, is a very complex one. During this phase, you need to put aside timidity and pessimism — but you can't be carefree and cavalier either. The correct traits to aim for, as you charge yourself up in front of the mirror each morning, are these: optimism, determination, and methodicalness.

Marketing Yourself

First, you will want to consider all the ways you can possibly market yourself. For example, a woman I know who recently received her Ph.D. in social psychology and is currently on the academic job market, was bemoaning the scarcity of positions in that area. However, though her degree was in social psychology, she had done much of her research on women's issues and is also a superb methodologist who has taught statistics to undergraduates. In addition, her research on women's fear of success is really in the realm of personality psychology, an area in which she has also taught undergraduate courses. What she might therefore reasonably consider herself qualified for would be teaching appointments specializing, not only in mainstream social psychology, but also in women's studies, research methodology and statistics, and personality psychology. Looking beyond psychology, she might very well be a desirable candidate in a *sociology* department seeking to hire an assistant professor specializing in sex roles in society and/or research methodology, if her social psychology training, in fact, had included sociological as well as psychological theory and method. And if she decided to emphasize her current postdoctoral work, which involves research on women's life-span development, she might also be a viable candidate for positions in departments of human development.

My own training is another case in point. I received my Ph.D. in social psychology, held a three-year predoctoral traineeship in cross-cultural child development (which included a dissertation on Mexican families), and did a predoctoral and postdoctoral clinical internship with special emphasis on family therapy and ethnicity and mental health. I was at first hired for a one-year position teaching personality psychology, and then later seriously considered for jobs in clinical, community, personality, and developmental psychology, in ethnic studies, and in family and sex roles in several sociology departments. Though I also did apply for mainstream social psychology jobs — none of which, to my knowledge, seriously considered me — by that time I was no longer very interested in that area and was glad to be able to move in other directions.

Access to Current Employment Information

Once you decide the areas in which you may be marketable, the second step is to gain continued access to information about available jobs. This means regularly checking the advertising sources for each of the fields you are considering. My friend, for example, should read the ads in the *APA Monitor* each month, send for the sociology *Employment Bulletin* put out monthly by the American Sociological Association, check APA's Division 35 (Psychology of Women) Newsletter whenever it comes out, and perhaps check the ads in *American Home Economics Action* and the *Chronicle of Higher Education* for human development-related jobs. Further, academic departments receive letters announcing new positions, even before they are publicly advertised. Thus my friend should, each month, look through the job notices and letters received by the psychology, sociology, and human development departments at her university.

Conferences are yet another good source of job listings, though the time of year influences what kinds of jobs will be available. Conferences held in the spring or summer are more likely to list temporary appointments for a last-minute replacement or a late-funded position. In the latter instance, a department will seek to hire a temporary person, in order to be able to do a thorough job search with a full crop of new candidates during the coming academic year. Fall, winter, and early spring conferences are more likely to offer tenure-track positions. The job I currently hold was obtained by registering my credentials with the employment service of a regional conference — one of two offers resulted from my attending.

Preparing Your Vita: The Chameleon Caper

The third step is the preparation of your vita. This is a crucial instrument, because it is what gets you past the first screening, identified as a serious contender. Your vita tells search committee members whether your qualifications are in the right area, and whether your experience and productivity are at the level that they intend to consider. You can get a general idea of a vita's overall structure by asking the junior faculty in your department if you can look theirs over. And when you prepare yours, make sure it is letter perfect and crisply printed. Beyond that, there are several basic things to know about preparing a vita, plus a few fancy ones. The basics are described below.

Include all work experience, publications, presentations, organizations, and committees that can be made to sound relevant to your professional image. This means the "research assistantship studying parent-infant interaction" when you helped out a faculty member one summer by doing some videotaping, or the "invited colloquium" when your friend invited you to present your dissertation findings at the monthly brown-bag lunch in her department. Try to list your most impressive and relevant qualifications first. Since job experience, publications, and presentations are listed chronologically, this will usually mean presenting your most recent accomplishments first, and working backwards.

Leave out any accomplishments before graduate school, unless they are important academic honors or serious work experiences. Include only those work experiences that are related to your profession — unless they somehow enhance your desirability. For example, if you spent three years as a concert pianist, or as a player on the professional tennis circuit, that might impress some people, and shouldn't hurt. Three years as a secretary or an insurance adjuster will simply come across as nonprofessional clutter. I included one four-year job teaching college English when I applied for academic positions in psychology, because it conveyed that I had both teaching experience and writing ability. However, I did not mention the one-year and summer positions I had also held, or the unpublished novel that was my Masters thesis.

Leave out papers that are "in preparation." Since this can mean anything from having an idea for a paper to just needing to have the final draft typed, search committee members tend to distrust and dismiss such listings. Better to include a description of the research itself in a separate statement of research interests.

Leave out indications of your age and marital or family status. Many folks out there still have preconceptions about older (or younger) women, married women, divorced women, and women with children. Keep them guessing. You should also take what steps are necessary to have such details removed from any official documents that might be sent to places where you are applying. For example, I had to petition my graduate university to get the dates of my B.A. and M.A. degrees removed from my graduate school transcript. You may in fact want to use some of that information to your advantage later on, when you have a job offer in hand and are negotiating terms (which will be discussed in a later section); however, at this early stage you should be careful not to activate any biases.

More fancy maneuvers for preparing your vita may be no less essential — in fact, they may be the key to getting you through the first gate, into serious consideration as a candidate. Specifically, if you are trying to sell yourself to several different markets, you need to have a suitable version of your vita for each one. I had five different mix-and-match versions of my vita, with up to four different versions of each page. For example, if I were applying for a social psychology or sociology position, the first page specified that my Ph.D. was in social psychology and gave the name of my advisor, who is well-known in both those fields. On the other hand, if I were applying for a position in clinical, community, developmental, or personality psychology, I used a first page that gave the department that awarded the degree (Psychology and Social Relations), without specifying the program. Similarly, my vita that was sent in application for nonclinical jobs left out all mention of my predoctoral clinical internship, and the description of my postdoctoral appointment was as follows: *Program emphasized awareness of cultural and family dynamics in the delivery of mental health services to ethnic minorities.* For jobs in clinical and community psychology, however, my vita spelled out the details of my predoctoral internship and, in addition to specifying that it was a *clinical* appointment, said the following about my postdoc: *Program included training in individual, group, and family therapy, assessment, outreach, crisis intervention, child protective work, and case management, in a multi-ethnic community setting.*

My listing of research and teaching interests, of course, varied with each version, as did the professional experiences I chose to list; the ordering within those listings varied accordingly as well. For example, some of the teaching interests I listed in my sociology vita were Social Psychology, Women and Sex Roles, Family in Cross-Cultural Perspective, and Social/Ethnic Issues and Mental Health. The teaching interests in my developmental psychology vita, however, included Developmental Psychology, Family Interaction and Parent-Child Relations, Sex Differences in Socialization, and Socioemotional Development.

In short, I left out of each version of my vita what I believed a search committee in that area would find irrelevant, or even questionable, and described my interests and accomplishments in a way that would as much as possible fit with the area I was applying to. I learned that this was necessary from my first year on the job market, when I had had one version of my vita that included everything. Feedback from confused and dubious search committees that first year made it clear that it was *not* a good idea — they saw me as unfocused and undecided in my career direction, and doing some pretty irregular things for a promising young scholar in their area. Being interdisciplinary was definitely not an advantage. In the minds of search committees, and the hiring departments behind them, breadth of training, experience, and interest was a dangerous thing, and candidates revealing such on their vita were to be regarded with suspicion.

Using Your Contacts

Once the application process is in motion, it is time to enlist the help of the contacts and networks you have been establishing. Call or send a note to each person you feel might be willing to be of help, explaining the kind of position you are seeking, and enclosing a version of your vita that is appropriate to the kind of job they might help you gain access to. Ask for their general advice — and for specific suggestions, if you think they may have influence at a particular place you are interested in. They may offer to make a phone call on your behalf to a former student who is now on the faculty there, or to send in your vita with a note attached, calling special attention to you as a worthwhile candidate. Now is not the time to be timid or shy. People will help if they can (and want to), and if they can't or don't, nothing has been lost in the asking.

Making Choices and Monitoring the Process

If you package yourself in a variety of ways, so that you can apply for academic positions in more than one discipline, you can substantially increase your chances of getting a suitable job. Given the reality that the chances of getting any one job are slim, it is important that you apply widely, for jobs that seem perfect for you, jobs you think you would probably be pleased with, and jobs you might possibly consider. In my case, because I had so many areas in which I was applying, my credentials were sent to approximately 90 places my final job search year (this is where two of those traits I mentioned earlier — optimism and determination —

were essential). Some of those places probably saw very little fit between their position and my qualifications — but I had at least 15 inquiries, 5 actual interviews, and 4 offers that year, and later learned that I had been among the final handful of candidates at a number of other places. Furthermore, a department's perception of fit can be hard to predict; a case in point is that the 4 offers I received were all from clinical or community psychology programs — and I had never taken a course or done research in either of those areas. Apparently my internships, teaching experience, and particular research interests made me a viable candidate in those situations and, fortunately for me, that was also my first choice for my career direction. If I had to do it again, the one thing I would do differently would to be more selective in terms of my own preferences; all it took was one interested phone call from one of the CUNY colleges, for example, for me to realize that I would not consider living in or near New York City.

However, whether you apply to 20 places or a hundred, it is important to do it *in a systematic way* (if you remember, methodicalness was the third essential trait I mentioned). This will both save you time and prevent your applications from being eliminated from consideration because some of your credentials were not submitted by the appropriate deadline. The most efficient way I know of to keep track of all aspects of all your applications is to keep a notebook. This should be of the looseleaf variety, so that information can be added or shifted around as you apply to more places. Make yourself 50 (or however many jobs you anticipate applying for) copies of a basic information sheet, which has a blank corner to attach a job ad that you clip from a newpaper or listing sheet. It should provide a space for the name and address of the person and place you are sending your credentials to, and list, in chronological order, all the steps of the application process, with a space next to each to put the date on which each step was completed. The list might look something like this:

Date
_____ Vita Version # ____ Sent
_____ Letters Requested From Referees
_____ Letter From _____ Sent
_____ Letter From _____ Sent
_____ Letter From _____ Sent
_____ Papers/Reprints Sent:

_____ Additional Materials Sent:

_____ Application Acknowledged
_____ Invited for Interview _____   Job Offered _____
_____ Rejection Received
Additional Comments and Information:

Keep these basic information sheets in alphabetical order by schools, along with a copy of the cover letter that accompanied them, any communication from the department applied to, and any additional relevant material. Finally, to save time, select several representative cover letters to be used as models for different types of jobs, so that successive ones need only be modified to the extent of pointing out how your qualifications fit closely with the advertised job description.

In this way you will be able to keep track of every aspect of the application process and to follow up on anything that seems amiss — for example, to call a place you are interested in if you haven't received acknowledgment of your application within a reasonable amount of time, or to get verbal acknowledgment from your referees that they have indeed sent their letters. One last point: promptness is important, in that many places do not wait until their specified closing date to start considering candidates, and may make an unofficial choice well before that time. Thus it is to your advantage to get your application in as soon as possible, and not delay until the deadline given in the ad.

THE NEXT STAGE: GOING FOR AN INTERVIEW

The Preparation Phase

If you have carried out enough of the preceding steps, and have applied to enough places, you should receive at least a few phone calls inviting you to come for a formal interview. This almost always means that you are among a department's top five candidates, and in fact are probably among the top three. You can ask the search committee chair how many people they have already interviewed and are planning to interview for the position. In order to know more of what to expect, you can also ask what about your qualifications especially interests their department, and what, if anything, are their questions or reservations about. In addition, you can ask to be sent any relevant information about their department or graduate program.

The search committee chair may be able to provide you with an advance list of whom you will be talking with, and you may wish to find out a little about each person, particularly anyone whose area might be related to yours. However, I found that it was unnecessary to do much advance homework; no one really expects you to be familiar with their work, and people are generally very pleased to tell you all about it. On the other hand, it is a good idea to find out what you can about the institution and the department from your own faculty members and contacts, including the department's reputation, its theoretical/research orientation, its politics, and any potential supporters or challengers. And it is also useful to request in advance to talk with some of the department's junior faculty (particularly the women), to learn about the department, the university, and the locale from their perspective. Most places with graduate programs provide opportunities to talk with graduate students as well, but it's not a bad idea to ensure that by requesting it in advance.

If you have several interview opportunities, be sure to arrange to go to the one you are *least* interested in first. This will be your chance to polish your colloquium delivery and to practice sounding intelligent, charming, and enthusiastic through a day or two of back-to-back half-hour meetings with just about everyone. My first time out, I had 17 meetings with different people, including during each meal. If your first interview is less important than the ones to follow, you can regard it more as a learning experience and be more relaxed as your feel your way along. Even so, you should prepare very thoroughly for the following things.

First, the colloquium (or brief oral presentation of your scholarly work) is of prime importance. Not only will it be evaluated for the content, but your style of delivery will be evaluated as an indicator of your teaching ability. Thus it is important that the talk be well-organized, engaging, and confidently presented. If you have never given such a talk, get advice on how to structure it from faculty members who are effective teachers, and attend talks within your department, using a critical eye to see what engages and impresses the audience and what doesn't. If you are presenting your research, make sure the methodological details and the results are very clearly laid out using professional-looking overhead transparencies or slides, and handouts if they are helpful. Pick out the most interesting or important findings, leaving out all the lesser details that might only serve to confuse your audience. Where possible, liven the talk by including anecdotal material that is humorous or engaging; for example, you can present interesting examples from interview protocols or describe some of the problems encountered in collecting the data. Give a practice talk in your department, invite the most critical faculty members, and tape the talk (and the feedback) so that you can work on them afterwards. See if you can prepare for questions that might arise, and have ready several nondefensive, stock responses to deal with the more difficult or challenging ones (e.g., "That's an interesting point, and I think it would be worth looking into," "That's an interesting point; however, I think it's more likely that . . . "You know, I hadn't thought of that — what do you think might be the reason?"). Work on developing an enthusiastic tone. And practice, practice, practice.

You will also need to put some attention on the courses you would be expected or would like to teach. Some departments have specific slots you will be expected to fill, but there is almost always some degree of choice as well. Get sample syllabi of those courses from your own faculty, or from friends and contacts at other institutions; in addition, many professional organizations provide teaching resources on request. Then come up with some rough course outlines of your own, so that you can sound knowledgeable and competent if anyone questions you about the courses you would be able to teach.

Finally, you will need to think about and be prepared to present a clear picture of the research that you intend to pursue. Departments seek new faculty who will plunge right into starting a research program (including applying for grants), and graduate departments seek faculty who will involve graduate students in their work. You may in fact not *know* precisely what kind of research you want to get involved in, but the point is to sound committed and prepared during the interview — even though you may end up doing something entirely different once you get the job.

Going On An Interview

When going on a long-distance interview, you can maximize your opportunities by calling any other schools you have applied to that are near or en route to where you are going, to see whether they might also be interested in talking with you (since it won't cost them anything). They may simply not be very far along in processing their applications, and your offer may push them to examine yours, to see whether they want to make use of the opportunity. Or it may turn out that though you were not in their top three candidates, you were in their top six, and so the search committee or department chair would like to look you over.

Some pointers about travel: First, do your best to get an economy-rate airline ticket. I actually had the experience of not getting an expected job offer because, through no fault of my own, I didn't buy the most economical ticket. The search committee, I later learned, decided that I obviously was not a very considerate person. Second, since long plane trips with rushed connections or long layovers can be stressful and tiring, try to arrange it so that you have some rest time after you arrive. Third, take only carry-on luggage. There is nothing more awkward than giving your colloquium in jeans and sneakers, or in wrinkled skirt and sweaty blouse, because your luggage never made it past Chicago. If you must check your luggage (perhaps because the interview is just one leg of a longer journey), make sure you carry your colloquium presentation materials with you, as well as the clothes you would need for one day and one night. And make sure you have comfortable shoes.

Once you arrive, remember that you are there to look them over, as well as vice versa. You are entitled to ask a lot of questions, about the program, the students, the teaching load, research assistance, secretarial help, computer facilities, research space, available funds for equipment, travel, and library books, and start-up money for beginning research. You will want to know something about the cost of housing, the climate, the quality of life there for a single (or married) junior faculty member — though at this phase of the process, I might avoid mentioning husband, and would certainly not mention having children. And you will want to know about the department and the university's hiring and retention practices. How often does a junior faculty member get reviewed for reappointment, and when does she or he come up for tenure? Have the junior faculty most recently hired been reappointed, and what percentage of eligible faculty has in fact gotten tenure? What are the bases for raises, reappointment, and tenure decisions — for example, how much emphasis is put on research, how much on teaching, and how much on service? How many women are in the department, and are they tenured or on tenure track? (See Checklist for the First Academic Job Search in Appendix.)

I began my first job, a one-year appointment at a prestigious women's college, having been told by the search committee chair that I would be in a good position to be considered for the tenure-track openings coming up for the following fall. What I didn't know was that that department had a history of cycling 10 new people through every year or two, in one-year, two-year, and part-time appointments. Five of the new people that year, after working as hard as they could to prove their mettle, applied for the three openings that became available — and not one was seriously considered. If I had had more specific information on the hiring and retention record of that department, I might still have accepted the one-year job, but I would not have directed so much physical and emotional energy toward an obviously unobtainable goal.

You will also be meeting with an administrator or two, most likely with the dean of the college. Here you will want to appear knowlegeable about larger academic issues. You can ask about faculty-administration relations — who sets academic policies, how are standards for raises, promotion, and tenure determined, what is the university record for tenuring faculty, and are there any special affirmative-action efforts underway? You can also ask about the future of the university, such as the effects of declining enrollments on admissions standards and faculty security, and plans for future expansion or development.

The truth is that aside from the tenseness and confusion of your very first exposure, going for academic job interviews can be fun. You are essentially the guest of honor, whom everyone wants to meet, talk to, and impress — and all that attention and interest can make you feel desirable, powerful, and important. You may get to know some pretty interesting people, and you may also make some useful professional contacts. Plus, you get a chance to get away from your everyday pressures and responsibilities (such as finishing your dissertation), perhaps to a beautiful campus, or a new city, or a scenic part of the country. If you do find yourself enjoying things, be sure to share that with your hosts, who will be delighted to hear how impressed you are with the research they are doing, the friendliness of the department, or the wonderful climate. The traits you will need to manifest at this time are confidence, knowledgeability (about your own area and work), interest (in everyone who interviews you), and enthusiasm.

REACHING THE END OF THE RAINBOW: THE JOB OFFER

When that magic moment arrives, the phone call from some department or search committee chair offering you a job, there may be a strong urge to say yes immediately. The sense of relief from knowing you won't end up jobless, plus the gratitude that somebody wants you, can be very compelling, leading you to close the door too soon to other possibilities, and to accept that first offer on whatever terms it is tendered. For these reasons, it is useful to have a few guidelines for yourself set up in advance, so that you can explore and maximize all opportunities.

First, unless you are sure that this is your number one choice, you should try to get at least several weeks to make your decision, with the deadline left as vague as possible. If they are pressing you to make a quick decision, you can say something like, "I'm really very interested in this position, but I also have some other possibilities that I'm waiting to hear about. I should be able to let you know in a few weeks." After that time, if you still aren't ready to make the decision, you may be able to stall for another week or two. In the meantime, you should request the offer in writing; a verbal offer from a department is not the same as an institution's written commitment to fund your position — and occasionally the discrepancy between the two has resulted in a candidate finding herself without an expected job, after turning down other offers.

In addition, now is the time to call all places that have shown an interest in you, to see whether they are still interested, as well as places you are interested in but haven't yet heard anything from. Tell these places that you have had an offer, and that you are calling to find out the status of your candidacy. Some of them may in fact be considering you, but haven't yet reached the final stages of the recruitment process. Your calling them may speed that up. And be sure, when you call, to speak to the department or search committee chair. A graduate student of mine, after receiving several offers, called the place she was most interested in but had heard nothing from to find out the status of her application. When she learned from the department secretary that the interviewing stage was underway and that she had not been selected as an interviewee, she accepted one of the offers she already had. Two weeks later, the department chair phoned to invite her to come for an interview — she had in fact been number four on their list. Clearly, had she spoken to the department chair when she called, she would have been given that information, and the chair would have found out that if they wanted to be able to consider her, they would have to act soon. Similarly, in two cases of my own where I was applying late, secretaries told me not to bother, that the search committees had already chosen the candidates they would be interviewing. I sent my credentials in anyway — and in one of those cases, I ended up with a job offer.

Negotiations

When you are fairly certain that you want a particular job that has been offered, then it is time to negotiate. The first thing you will want to negotiate is your salary. Find out what recently hired peers are receiving and go for the upper end of that range. It may be that that is in fact what is offered to you. But if not, there are at least four good reasons why you should try for the highest possible salary: (1) you will have more money for yourself, which can be especially helpful when you are relocating; (2) perceptions of a person's worth are affected by the amount of money she or he is paid — in other words, if you are paid more, people will think you are worth more; (3) the annual raise at your institution may be figured as a percentage of your current salary, so that it is to your advantage to start off at as high a level as possible; and (4) you will be recognized as someone to be reckoned with, rather than ignored or overlooked, when it comes to distributing departmental resources in the future.

There are a number of ways to negotiate for a salary higher than the one that has been offered. You can tell them that you appreciate their offer, but that you had in mind a salary more in the neighborhood of X thousand dollars. If you have reasons to bring up in support of your case, all the better — such as your two postdoctoral years, your extensive teaching experience, or your unusually high number of publications. I was able to negotiate higher salaries on several job offers by stressing my postdoctoral experience, my previous teaching experience (some of it in another field, and some of it nonacademic), and my general life experience, as a mature woman who was 10 years older than most other applicants, who could serve as a role model for female graduate students.

Another approach, if you have more than one job offer in hand, is to elaborate on how much you would really like to accept the present job offer, but that you have been offered (or are negotiating) a higher salary elsewhere, which would be difficult to turn down. You can quote that figure to show how much another place thinks you are worth. And if you are good at this sort of negotiation, you can do the same thing with two or more places, playing them off against one another. Difficult as it is for most women to believe, people respect you more (and do not like you less) when you go after a higher salary. And when you reach the limit of what they will pay in salary, then it is time to negotiate for other items, such as moving expenses (which can be several thousand dollars), a computer, laboratory equipment, seed money for research, and release from teaching time during the first year so that you can get your research started.

By the time departments reach a decision to offer a job to a particular candidate, often after a long search and some difficult political maneuvers both with the administration and within the department itself, they are eager to complete the process, and do not want to go through it all again. Thus you will often have more leverage than you realize when negotiating for what you want. They will not give up on you easily and will very likely make some accommodations.

OUTCOMES AND ALTERNATIVES

Generally you will know before the end of May whether or not you have found a suitable tenure-track position for the following fall. If you have, congratulations — now read the chapters by Gibbons, Quina, Rose, and Stake for how to survive the first few years in academia. If you haven't, you need to evaluate how well you did do, and what you may need to change or improve. First, it is a good idea to get specific feedback from some of the places where you applied. If you knew you were a serious contender for a particular job, or felt you should have been, call and ask the search committee chair (or anyone you happen to know in that department) how your candidacy was viewed. If nothing else, it will make you feel better about the form rejections you received to find out that you were in fact among the top 10 finalists at several places. Then, with the help of any feedback you receive, decide which aspects of your credentials you need to work on — such as submitting more papers for publication, cultivating contacts who will write wonderful recommendations for you, or getting more research or teaching experience in a particular area.

At this point, there are a number of different paths to take, all of which can help you move toward the kind of main track position you are seeking. The most common ones are postdocs and temporary research or teaching appointments. If you haven't applied (or have applied unsuccessfully) for a postdoctoral fellowship, it may still be possible to get one late in the academic year. While some are still being advertised, others are known only through private sources, so you will need to call on all your contacts. I learned about my postdoc in late spring, from a consultant at my clinical internship placement, whom I happened to sit next to at a picnic. Another postdoc offer came to me through a colleague of a faculty member in my department.

The same process applies for research and temporary teaching appointments. For the latter, however, you can go further. One-year positions are often listed at conferences or advertised late in the academic year, so you will want to make use of all available listing sources. In addition, if there are other academic institutions in your area, it is a good idea to send in your credentials, stating your interest in both full-time and part-time teaching. Then try to set up a meeting with the department chair, so that she or he will keep you in mind should a position become available, and call back in a few months to see if anything has opened up. If you already know someone in the department, or know someone who knows someone, that can also be helpful. Don't be hesitant to use whatever personal "pull" you can muster.

In any case, it is almost certain that something worthwhile will result. Our studies of women and men applying for academic jobs (Bronstein et al., 1986a, 1986b) showed that about 90% obtained full-time psychology-related jobs, and about 70% obtained full-time academic teaching positions, with less than 5% reporting unemployment. This additional year will give you an opportunity to sharpen your skills, enhance your credentials, and continue your quest for the ideal job. And while you will still experience the anxiety of the job-seeking process, you should make sure to enjoy what is probably your last year of freedom from the incredible pressures and stress of a tenure-track academic position.

REFERENCES

Brodsky, A. (1974). Women as graduate students. *American Psychologist*, 29, 523–529.

Bronstein, P., Black, L., Pfennig, J., & White, A. (1986a, in press). Stepping onto the academic ladder: How are women doing? In B. Gutek & L. Larwood (Eds.), *Pathways to women's career development*. Beverly Hills, CA: Sage Books.

Bronstein, P., Black, L., Pfennig, J., & White, A. (1986b, in press). Getting academic jobs: Are women equally qualified—and equally successful? *American Psychologist*, 318–321.

Ceci, S. J., & Peters, D. (1984). Letters of reference: A naturalistic study of the effects of confidentiality. *American Psychologist*, 39(1), 29–31.

Freeman, J. (1972). *How to discriminate against women without really trying.* Department of Political Science, University of Chicago.

Guillemin, J., Holmstrom, L. L., & Garvin, M. (1979). Judging competence: Letters of recommendation for men and women faculties. *School Review*, February, 157–170.

Hoffman, N. J. (1972). Sexism in letters of recommendation: A case for consciousness-raising. *Modern Language Association Newsletter, 4*, Winter, 4–5.

Holmstrom, E. T., & Holmstrom, R. (1974). The plight of the woman doctoral student. *American Educational Research Journal, 11,* 1–17.

Lewis, L. S. (1975). *Scaling the ivory tower: Merit and its limits in academic careers.* Baltimore: Johns Hopkins Press.

Lunneborg, P. W., & Lillie, C. (1973). Sexism in graduate admissions: The letter of recommendation. *American Psychologist, 28*(2), 187–189.

Schaffer, D. R., & Tomarelli, M. (1981). Bias in the ivory tower: An unintended consequence of the Buckley Amendment for graduate admissions. *Journal of Applied Psychology, 66,* 7–11.

Sells, L. (1973). *Sex differences in graduate school survival.* Paper presented at the annual meeting of the American Sociological Association, New York.

■ 2
Pitfalls on the Way to Tenure

JUDITH GIBBONS

As a junior faculty member, you are likely to have the best training, the greatest commitment to teaching, the most dedication, and the most innovative research of any member of your department. Yet when you apply for tenure, the criteria applied to you probably will be more stringent than your tenured colleagues faced. Moreover, these criteria may have shifted in their focus and are often unclearly defined. Therefore, it helps to approach the tenure process with a plan.

The tenure requirements can be broadly divided into two categories, the *formal* and the *informal*. These have been called the "contest" and "sponsorship" aspects of achieving tenure (Macaulay & Hall, 1984). Formally, the tenure process is an open contest in which a person wins by meeting established criteria. The formal criteria for tenure often are stated in a faculty manual. Informally, the tenure process is analogous to induction into a private club where one must be sponsored to enter. The criteria for entry are not explicit; frequently, they depend on personal characteristics and relationships. Informal criteria are implied in statements like, "She just doesn't fit in."

FORMAL REQUIREMENTS

The formal criteria for tenure most often include teaching, research, and service (Whitman & Weiss, 1982). These may be weighted differently, however, depending on the university, or on the school or department within the university. The formal criteria are likely to be written somewhere. Get a copy from the dean, the faculty manual, or the rank and tenure committee. If possible, get a list of the selection criteria actually used by the rank and tenure committee. Most often there is a rating form where different activities are rated and, perhaps, given weight. Find out as much about the formal process as you can. Where is it initiated? Who writes letters of recommendation to the committee? Which deans contribute to the process? Is there a university policy limiting the percentage of tenured faculty?

Discuss the formal criteria with friendly colleagues and, if possible, a member or ex-member of the rank and tenure committee. What do they think are the most important criteria? For example, although the criteria may include scholarly activities (research), teaching, advising, and service to the university, only research may actually affect the decision at a major university. A small college may have the same list of formal criteria, but may value teaching more highly. Service and advising are often difficult to assess and may contribute little to the decision.

Kasten (1984) studied the criteria used for tenure decisions at a large Midwestern research university. She presented a sample of tenured faculty members with profiles of hypothetical candidates for tenure. The quality and quantity of research were varied, and faculty were asked to make a tenure decision on the candidate. Both research and teaching significantly contributed to the decision, although research was significantly more important in the judgments. Faculty consistently stated that excellent research, including national or international recognition for scholarly contributions, could compensate for mediocre or even poor teaching. Faculty agreed that although teaching was less important than research, outstanding teaching could ameliorate the effects of an average research record. There was a consensus among faculty that service had no effect on tenure decisions. Every applicant could construct a case for adequate service to the department and university.

Although other institutions may assign somewhat different importance to these criteria, for many, research is the most significant and possibly the most variable criterion used. However, as college enrollments drop, I believe that both colleges and universities increasingly will demand serious scholarship from their faculty. Many institutions look for evidence of programmatic research from a tenure applicant, so develop an area in which you are an expert early in your career.

Take publishing seriously from the beginning. Jayne Stake, in this book, has provided some excellent advice on publishing, particularly on responding to feedback from potential publishers. Some additional issues include where to publish and what to publish. To determine the best publications in your area, start by reading the journals. Where do the best articles appear? Second, ask your colleagues what the best journals are (remember, however, that a journal's reputation may lag behind its actual quality). Third, find some critical articles in the field and look at the origin of their references. In what journals did their references appear? Your work may be judged by how often it is cited, so find out what periodicals or presses are cited most often. (There are some citation indexes where you can look this up: *Science Citation Index, Social Science Citation Index,* and *Arts and Humanities Citation Index.*) A fourth criterion for the quality of a journal is its rejection rate. Usually, publications with the highest rejection rates are considered the most prestigious.

A hotly debated issue is whether there are some places where you should not publish, or at least that you should not list on your vita. You need to look at the norms of your institution. What do other faculty do, and what do they recommend? At some institutions an article in a popular magazine is considered a plus; at others it is considered frivolous. Tenure applicants have included letters to the editor of newspapers as evidence of scholarship. At some institutions this would be poorly regarded. Publication in unrefereed journals is another area of debate. Make your decision about where not to publish based on the norms of your colleagues and of your profession.

As far as what to publish is concerned, you should concentrate first on your serious scholarship. Then don't neglect other possibilities. Publish a talk you gave at a symposium or workshop. If you design a new course, publish it in a teaching journal in your field. Publish a book of case studies, or edit a book of readings. Depending on your institution, these publications may contribute significantly to your credentials for tenure; they are unlikely to detract from your application.

How heavily teaching will be weighed depends on your institution. Whereas good teaching may not necessarily help you, complaints about your teaching or poor teaching evaluations may count against you. Even if it is not a requirement, it is a good idea to have students formally evaluate your courses and to keep the evaluations from each course you teach. Also keep laudatory comments on your teaching and thank-you notes from students.

If your teaching evaluations have been poor or mediocre, a good strategy is to ask for some teaching advice from other faculty. You might also evaluate your courses in the middle of the semester, and then try to respond to student criticism before the final evaluations occur. A classic reference on college teaching is *Teaching Tips* (McKeachie, 1978). If you think that your teaching evaluations unfairly represent your teaching, a bold strategy is to invite the department chair to one of your classes so she or he can evaluate you personally.

Service and advising may be the most time-consuming activities and also the most difficult to document in terms of quality. Moreover, they may contribute little to your meeting the formal criteria for tenure (Kasten, 1984). Nevertheless, as described below, your taking on responsibilities in the department and university may contribute to your reputation as a good citizen and significantly affect the informal criteria for tenure. Your responsibilities to the department will be extremely demanding. A partial list includes:

- Advising graduate and undergraduate students.
- Faculty evaluation of graduate students (may take two full days a semester).
- Serving on graduate students' preliminary examination, thesis, and dissertation committees.
- Graduate student recruitment and admissions.
- Designing graduate and undergraduate curricula.
- Attending undergraduate functions, including honorary societies, freshman orientation, and graduation ceremonies.

You will also be asked to serve the university on committees ranging from the curriculum committee to organizing graduation ceremonies. *Time* will be your biggest problem. Every committee needs a woman member, and you will be called upon disproportionately. It is important to serve on some university committees. Try to select those that are important and visible to the higher administration. Urge the committee to submit written reports, with your name in bold print.

The documentation of your efforts to meet the formal criteria is extremely important and has been described thoroughly in Quina's chapter.

INFORMAL REQUIREMENTS

The informal requirements for tenure are, of course, more difficult to specify. Several of the women with whom I talked suggested that some of these are best met by *choosing* a job at a place where you fit in. When you take a job, try to select an institution whose goals are consistent with your own. For example, I would find myself isolated at a Jesuit Catholic institution if I didn't feel that discussion of values and ethics were an important part of education. Some universities stress programmatic research, whereas others value collegiality above all else and would not be likely to promote a competitive person. A friend described her good fit at a university by saying, "This place is just kooky enough for me." Another expressed satisfaction at being at a college where there were already several tenured feminists.

Assuming you have chosen your university well, there are still pitfalls in meeting the informal requirements. One veteran of the tenure process described the importance of nonexplicit tenure criteria:

> My experience is that no one can get a positive recommendation from the faculty unless he or she is well-liked. Faculty who are well-liked will have a solid case constructed for them by other faculty. This is assuming, of course, a fairly good record in teaching, scholarship, and community service. Someone who is well-liked can have minimal scholarship and be a good teacher and get a tenure recommendation. Someone who is not well-liked will have a negative case constructed against them, no matter how "objectively" strong the person's record.
>
> Now what does well-liked mean? Not being abrasive and pushy; having some good friends among the tenured faculty; carrying one's load in the department so that others aren't unfairly burdened; being a fun person to have lunch with; having similar values. I believe that women have a harder time [than men] achieving this elusive quality of being "well-liked." Another way of saying this is that men have more latitude — they can be abrasive at times and they do less shit work.

Another veteran similarly noted the crucial social component of acceptance:

> I was at a small liberal arts college. There are two things I know now which I wish I'd known then. One is the importance of being political, of knowing where the power lies and making an effort to be personable in those quarters. I think I couldn't tell the difference between personable and ingratiating, and I refuse to be the latter.
>
> Second, and much more important, is that I had no idea I was in any trouble. I was relying on someone to tell me, and no one I was close to had any idea either. All the concrete, supposedly objective things like teaching evaluations were positive. What I didn't understand was the importance of "gossip" (I don't know what else to call it) between students and faculty at a small college. A lot of powerful faculty had "heard" that I was cold and did not relate well to students. That may have meant two faculty

members and four students, but I had no idea, and I really did not think to make in-depth inquiries until it was too late. I should not have taken *anything* for granted.

While it may not protect you from a negative tenure decision, my advice is to make some effort to be collegial, political, and likeable without being ingratiating. Without sacrificing your values or self-esteem, attend to the unwritten expectations of the other faculty members. Are you expected to lunch with the boys and drink beer on Friday afternoons? If you can be congenial and attend these informal gatherings, do it. Learn to play poker, raquetball, or tennis, if those are faculty activities. Do as much to make your case as you feel comfortable doing. After a negative tenure decision at the level of the president of the university, one applicant simply introduced herself to the president at a social function. When her case came up again, he had met the person behind the application papers. Her second tenure application was successful.

PROBLEMS FOR WOMEN

One problem uniquely affecting women faculty is their underrepresentation in the university and concentration in the lower ranks, as noted in the chapter by Yoder. This creates a situation in which women often are "tokens" within their department. Kanter (1977, 1980) studied the effects of being a token representative of a group and has suggested that some of women's experiences in academe are due to their minority status. She has described these experiences vividly.

Tokens, termed *O*'s by Kanter, stand out more than the majority members (*X*'s). This increased visibility leads to more gossip about women, as described in the personal account above. Furthermore, *O*'s are subjected to increased scrutiny, which is related not to their job performance, but to their *O-ness*. A frequently repeated comment by male members of one department was, "I saw you women having lunch together again — what are you plotting now?"

Kanter also has described how, when in the presence of a token, majority group members remind the token of their higher status either directly or indirectly. An assistant professor described the conversations at the faculty lunch table where she was a token woman. When she arrived, the conversation turned to sports and car repairs. For black women, as

Barnes and Banks mention in their chapters, tokenism is likely to be experienced along both race and sex dimensions.

Tokens also suffer from lack of sponsors (fewer women are available to help them), stereotyping, and competition with other women for the few women's positions. Kanter states that having two of a minority group does not often help; one is labeled the good *O* and the other is labeled the bad *O*.

Kanter (1980) recommends that tokens be aware of the situational factors which make people act as they do. She also suggests developing competence and finding ways to demonstrate that competence. Some of her suggestions are similar to those described above: learn to be diplomatic and to have a sense of humor. Finally, she suggests that women share coping strategies with other women.

A woman's attributions for her success or failure also may stand in the way of a successful academic career. If a woman attributes her successes to external factors such as luck or ease of task, and her failures to internal factors such as lack of ability, she may set herself up for defeat. One woman who was denied tenure wrote to me about her feelings of failure:

> In terms of the aftermath, it took at least two years for me to recover from the ego damage. I felt that I had been a failure. And yet I did not know how to attribute my failure. That is, what exactly was wrong with me? The support of close friends and colleagues in terms of attributing the problem to the school and not to me was very important in the healing process.

This woman gives us clues as to ways to combat this attributional tendency. With the help of friends, take pride in your successes. Attribute your accomplishments to your own skill and competency. To some extent, attribute your failures to the situation. One woman explained her failure to get a particular job in a way that maintained her self-esteem, "They really wanted someone with a different research area from mine."

Lastly, women faculty may be viewed as less credible scholars than men, particularly if their scholarship focuses on women. Sexism is present to a certain extent even in relatively benign settings. One commenter wrote about her university: 'Feminist scholarship is fairly well-respected [here], although I believe it is harder for someone doing *radical* feminist research to be promoted to full professor." You might be aware of the presence of sexism, without necessarily changing your area of research.

IF YOU ARE DENIED TENURE

If you are denied tenure you will feel angry, frustrated, and hurt. Don't do anything immediately; wait until you can think more clearly. Then try to assess the situation. Will you have another opportunity to apply for tenure? Not all institutions are "up or out." You may be eligible to apply again, or you may have the option of staying on a nontenure line. (Note that the American Association of University Professors does not recognize alternatives to tenure, although they are becoming more common.)

In assessing the reasons for your denial of tenure, try to get the best information possible. Contact the person who sent your denial letter; that person should explain the reasons for the decision. Try as best you can to evaluate the information. Is there something you can change to have a better chance next time? This may involve just waiting a year until you are more senior, doing more research, or serving on more committees. One woman was granted tenure the second time she applied; the first application was turned down since she had been at the university only a brief time, and her department was "overtenured." At the time of her second application, these factors had changed.

It is possible that nothing you can do will get you tenure at that institution. There seem to be two predominant responses to a negative decision, either over- or under-attribution of responsibility. As pointed out above, women are more likely to feel that there is something wrong with them. The opposite response, attributing full blame to the institution, might not be helpful if it blinds you to areas that you might change. Even if you are unsuccessful at that university, you might well use the information you have gained to help you get tenure elsewhere.

When you get a negative tenure decision and cannot reapply, there are still many options. You may want to file a grievance, look for another academic job, or leave academe altogether (see chapters by Gore, Larwood, and Shepela). Use the contacts you made when you sent your work to outside evaluators for your tenure review to track down job opportunities.

And if you receive tenure. . . . Congratulations, you deserve it.

REFERENCES

Kanter, R. M. (1977). Some effects of proportions on group life: Skewed sex ratios and responses to token women. *American Journal of Sociology*, 82, 965–990.

Kanter, R. M. (1980). *A tale of "O:" On being different in an organization.* New York: Harper & Row.

Kasten, K. L. (1984). Tenure and merit pay as rewards for research, teaching, and service at a research university. *Journal of Higher Education, 55,* 500–511.

Macaulay, J., & Hall, E. R. (1984, May). *How to get tenure even if you're a woman.* Paper presented at the Midwest Regional Association for Women in Psychology Conference, Ann Arbor, MI.

McKeachie, W. J. (1978). *Teaching tips: A guidebook for the beginning college teacher* (7th ed.). Lexington, MA: Heath.

Whitman, N., & Weiss, E. (1982). *Faculty evaluation: The use of explicit criteria for promotion, retention, and tenure.* (AAHE–ERIC/Higher Education Research Report No. 2, 1982). Washington, DC: National Institute of Education. (ERIC Document Reproduction Service No. ED 221 148.)

■ 3
Helping Yourself to Tenure

KATHRYN QUINA

This is not an advice column that reads "Publish, publish publish." Academics hear that every day, and most of us spend many of our waking hours either doing that or feeling anxious about doing it. This chapter instead addresses some informal and formal actions we can take to help ourselves through that dreaded hurdle of the mandatory tenure decision. As you may already suspect, publishing is necessary but not sufficient in most academic environments. Even the most outstanding candidate benefits from a good, strong presentation of herself and her achievements.

TIMING

The First Review

Most departments do some sort of review at the end of your first full year. If not, ask your Chair for feedback (written, if possible). While your contract may not be under consideration, this first review is an important one, as it "sets the tone" for future reviews. Try to get any articles in progress prepared prior to the first review deadline so you can include them. Prepare your dossier carefully and append relevant materials: publications, prepublication drafts, research proposals, and grant proposals. Evidence that you are forming a research team (including students) is another good first-year accomplishment, particularly if you are in the social or natural sciences. Include your teaching evaluations and comments, and any letters you have received commenting on your work or thanking you for service. Don't worry about including too much material, as long as you are not redundant and everything you append is relevant.

React to a negative evaluation immediately. If you know that a colleague has commented unfavorably on your work, talk to him or her. It may be painful, but you will establish in that person's eyes your willingness to work on your weaknesses. Ask for specific tactics for improvement, such as "How do you select the right journal?" If there are inaccuracies in the evaluation, straighten them out.

If any evaluations passed forward or placed in your file are incorrect or inappropriate, meet them with one or more of the following actions:

1. Ask the original evaluator to correct inaccuracies in a followup letter, and make sure that she or he does so.

2. Write a response to your evaluation, documenting the inaccuracies.

3. Talk to other junior faculty; you may find one person giving unkind evaluations to everybody. One year a colleague rated every profeminist (male or female) as "unsuited to this department." In such a case, you might consider group action to have that person's evaluations removed or passed forward "in context."

4. Check your contract; in some cases faculty have successfully overturned negative decisions or removed materials from their files through union or other grievance actions. At the very least, colleagues will be more hesitant to submit unfair evaluations if they know you are willing to file a grievance.

5. Assess yourself at this time, too. If you seem to have difficulty getting that research written up, or if your teaching evaluations are low, seek out help now. Find a mentor, such as a journal editor or a good teacher, and work on your rough spots.

Third-year Review

This midpoint is perhaps the best time to ask the tough questions:

Do I have a chance at tenure in this department? If all your evaluations have been negative, and you cannot possibly meet the standards placed before you (fair or not), devote some energy to writing a good resume and start searching. You are in a far better bargaining position with other schools now than as a "last-year desperate tenure turn-down." Besides, you have some time to look (four years, to be exact).

Do I want to stay at this place? Even if you are in good standing, if you do not like your colleagues or your environment, this is the time to consider moving. If you do not like teaching or research or some other critical aspect of your job, then it is definitely time to move—to a more satisfying career!

Do I have grounds for legal action? If you are uncertain about your department's opinion of you, but feel you have been the victim of discrimination of any form, collect your materials and consult a lawyer now. You may not wish to take any action at this time, but you will have a better perspective on your options and a better case later on.

This is also the time to get your national network going. (For suggestions concerning how to do so, see the chapter by Rose.) It will help if people well-known in the field know you and your work; they may be asked to write letters of evaluation for you.

As with the first review, react to any unfair or negative evaluations swiftly and strongly.

The Fifth Year

Review all prior evaluations carefully. If you have not met all the legitimate criticisms, set your goals for your sixth year accordingly. Decide on your priorities according to the assessments you have received. Devote your energy to getting the best record possible, and turn down unimportant activities for now. Tell everybody you are getting ready for tenure; they will understand.

The Decision Year

Start early. Get your dossier together in time to request your outside letters at least a month in advance. Plan into your schedule time for "extras" during the decision period as well. It is not unusual to get last-minute requests from deans or higher-level committees for extra information, revisions, or additional letters.

ASSESSING YOUR STANDING

It is often difficult to get a realistic assessment of your chances for tenure on the basis of formal feedback and verbal comments. These are subject to overemphasis of your weaknesses (administrators don't seem to know about the value of positive feedback); overvaluation of your colleagues' accomplishments (especially those of the person telling them); and overestimation of the difficulty of getting tenure (especially among those who already have it). Instead of relying on those sources, collect a perspective on the tenure standards in your university, using the following resources.

Written records of colleagues: Who else has received tenure recently in your department? In comparable other departments? What have they accomplished? How did they state their cases? Ask them if you can see their promotion dossiers. Each time someone is up for review, examine the department's reactions. Then evaluate your own strengths using the same criteria. Standards get a little tougher each year, but matching or bettering your tenurable colleagues constitutes a reasonable standard for yourself.

Conversations with supportive colleagues: What do they see as your strengths and weaknesses? Can they suggest ways to capitalize on your strength (e.g., research awards, funded consortiums you can join)? Can you rely on them for support during the tenure decision process, even if it gets rough?

Contacts with knowledgeable people in the university: A positive recommendation from your department is only one step in the decision process. What do deans, university review boards, and others who will be evaluating your promotion expect? If you have a union or faculty organization, talk to them beforehand about the process, about grievances, and about past experiences.

PREPARING YOUR CASE

Like a lawyer in the courtroom, you have to present a case in favor of your promotion. It is not only your right, but your responsibility to make it appealing to your jury. Forget the old wisdom about being modest. Don't downplay your accomplishments or your national reputation because bragging doesn't meet academic decorum. Don't expect colleagues to "fill in" missing data to make you better than your underplayed written record. You have to present yourself as the most deserving person they will view this year, so swallow your modesty, and let them know how competent and how important to them you are.

Attitude

Develop your dossier with a positive attitude. Examine your strengths, and list the ways in which you make unique contributions to your students, your department, and your field. I found it helpful to talk to a few colleagues, who listed contributions and strengths I hadn't recognized. I simply asked them "Why do I deserve tenure?"

Revise Any Self-critical Thinking

It doesn't matter if you haven't met all your personal goals, or if you feel you haven't done everything you wanted to. Tenure and promotion are based on what you have done relative to others. What could be seen as flaws by some can even be revised to your advantage in the eyes of others. For example, early reviews suggested that my switch in research areas would be seen as scattered and unfocused. On the advice of a wise colleague, I campaigned on my ability to make contributions in two disparate areas ("not just one like most people"). Not only was this positive approach reflected in better evaluations, it also helped me think better of myself.

Appearance

Your dossier should be well-organized and neat. Your vita should be professional and accurate; even typographical errors set a bad tone. Your whole record should be laid out in orderly fashion, easy to follow, and faithful to your university's format and standards. I even took some lessons from those vaccuum cleaner sales pitches. One of the best investments I made was 20 dollars for a large ring binder with envelope pages for papers and plastic page covers for letters and documents. If your department frowns upon a plastic case, the remaining principles apply nevertheless.

I created a "pattern of impressions" with my ring-bound record, subtly directing the reader's attention to the credentials I wished to emphasize. I began with a cover letter and my vita, with each page numbered and encased in plastic. These were followed by appendixes containing documentation, organized by section (research, teaching, service), each section starting with the strongest point. Noteworthy items got their own page or pocket, while others could be grouped. Everything was clearly labeled to prevent displacement. This "notebook" approach allowed greater control over the special cases I was making, since evaluators were most likely to start at the beginning and work through in the order I wanted, and to divide their attention in the way I mapped out for them in the documentation. Nothing was lost, or became disordered, and colleagues were pleased by the relative ease of the usually onerous task of plowing through loose and detached pages.

Make a copy of everything you submit and keep it in a safe place in case you need to replace pages. Check your dossier periodically while it is available to colleagues for review. Even with your best efforts items can be torn, misplaced, or not returned. Years ago after I was criticized by a colleague for having done no research, I discovered too late that a portion of my dossier had been lost. To add to my woes, I had to retype the whole section, and others were inconvenienced by the delay.

DOSSIER CONTENTS

While local customs vary, the following should provide a model of the minimum contents of your dossier.

Cover Letter

You should set the tone of your case with an opening statement in which you: (1) stress your strengths, including your contributions to the field of psychology; (2) explain your value to the department, defining the crucial and unique roles you fill; and (3) define the major reasons you deserve tenure. Answer any potential criticisms, directly or indirectly, but be firm in your conviction that you are the best person for this promotion. About two pages is a good length.

Vita

This is not an ordinary brief resume; it is a complete accounting of everything you have accomplished over the past six years. Don't be redundant or "bullish"; that ploy is annoying to your readers. But don't leave out anything because it seems "small" or "long ago." I've seen promotion vitae that list every talk to every community group, every convention attended. While I prefer summaries of that sort of activity, it is evidence of your professional involvement and should be included. Other items frequently forgotten are new courses developed, guest lectures in others' classrooms, instructional development such as workshops attended, and student advising.

Incorporate evaluations of your work into the vita, where possible. If your department chair or committee disapproves of that practice, place evaluations in another conspicuous location. When you list classes taught, include a summary evaluation statement if possible (e.g., the line "mean rating 4.2 on a 5- point scale" will fit nicely below the course data). When your publications are listed, add a sentence or two about the significance of the work, and don't be coy about using the word "I" (e.g., "This was the first demonstration of the Keebler Effect with elves under in vitro conditions. Subsequent work in the area has relied heavily on the methodology I developed."). Below each publication, add a line for Citations (the number will suffice, though if the citation is in a major review, you might wish to list the citation source). Citations of your work can be obtained at your library, using the citation indexes, and are probably available at little cost from their computerized search services. If you have received commendations for any work, list them along with the work (e.g., Psi Chi Letter of Appreciation, 1978, for support of student research).

If you have been involved with significant publications on which you are not an author but you are footnoted or otherwise recognized (get a letter!), you should include a section listing those works, clearly labeled as works to which you made contributions. However, do not overemphasize or make this section too lengthy.

Supporting Letters from Outside Evaluators

These are perhaps the most important part of your record, because senior faculty tend to rely on the evaluations of others in your field to determine your level of or potential for national recognition. If your efforts at networking for the past few years have worked, you may have met your evaluators or worked with them on committees or projects. If you have some control over the names picked for outside evaluation, choose members of your network with credentials your colleagues can recognize.

If you are required to obtain letters yourself, request them well in advance. Send potential evaluators your cover letter, your vita, and copies of relevant materials to be evaluated. Let them know the points you would like them to stress. Make the process as easy as possible for the reviewer; extras like addressed, stamped envelopes can be time-saving. Request more letters than are required, and follow up to make sure the minimum number are received.

Letters from people you have been closely affiliated with, such as your major professor, may be good supplements, but will not be accepted in place of the outside reviews. Letters from students are helpful in setting a positive tone, but should not appear to be solicited. Letters from former students who have achieved professional status of their own are also useful, especially if they stress your guidance as a researcher. But in these cases, don't overdo it; more than two or three letters begins to suggest a "campaign."

Documentation

Copies of all teaching evaluations, publications, papers, letters, and so on, should be appended to your vita. Letters specifically commenting on a paper should be "packaged" with that paper; reviews of books with that book, and so on. The rule of thumb is "orderly and organized." In my vita I referenced specific sections (e.g., "See Appendix A"), and labeled the documentation pages or folders accordingly.

If you would like to describe specific activities in greater detail than a vita permits (e.g., administrative responsibilities or accomplishments of a particular committee), you can include such information as an appendix in the documentation section as well. Let importance to your case and ease of flow for the reader be your guides in deciding what goes in an appendix as opposed to in the vita.

DECISION OUTCOMES

A Negative Vote

In spite of their outstanding records and their best efforts to present their case, some very competent people are turned away without tenure. The process has its irrational outcomes, and often they are most unfair to women. If this happens to you, do all of the following.

File a grievance. Even if your grievance is turned down, taking action is better than remaining silent. You should still have another chance for a positive vote next year. If you have not linked up with your faculty organization and your academic/professional women's organization by now, make up for your omissions by paying your dues and networking. You will find support, and you may find others with whom to file a class action suit. Such a suit will certainly help future women, if not yourself.

Get your vita into circulation. Even if you don't want to leave, your case next year will be much stronger if you have an alternative in hand. There's nothing like someone else wanting you to make your own team want you more. In fact, you may find another location or team that is better. I have a friend who was fired unfairly, and entered the job market unwillingly, who became the Chair at another university with an $11,000 salary increase and is still happily there.

Keep up your morale. You are in good company; some of the best scholars in the country have been victims of unfair tenure decisions. Of course, being turned down is disrupting, disturbing, and frightening; those effects are genuine and reasonable. But you must avoid the tendency to believe that you are a failure or unqualified, or that it is the "end of your career." Instead, redirect your energy toward your future options, looking forward to finding people who will appreciate your work.

Tenure Granted — Congratulations!

Now, what do you do? First, remember that lots of people experience the imposter phenomenon. I had nightmares for several months after my promotion that the administration discovered I really didn't deserve it, and they arrived at my home to take it back. If you were positively evaluated by all those people, you earned your promotion, so enjoy the recognition you deserve.

Second, don't forget to thank everybody who helped you along the way. Your supporters will be pleased to have you recognize their efforts.[1]

Third, don't look at tenure as the "end" of the process. Rather, it is the time for opportunities to grow and for you to do the rich research and

[1] In that spirit of appreciation, I would like to thank the faculty women of the University of Rhode Island, whose brave lawsuit made the difference for some who followed; my supportive colleagues (especially Bernice, Jan, and Al) who let me "start over" at a second job after a lousy first experience and who convinced me I was worthy of the Associate Professor level; and my husband David, who brought his experience in marketing into the ivory towers and who helped sell me on myself in the process.

thinking you put off before. It means you can speak up more freely, taking controversial positions and supporting other women even more strongly than before. A tenured feminist can make a difference! Take a vacation to bask in your new status, and then take a new step forward to help your department continue to become a better environment for everyone.

■ 4
Building a Professional Network

SUZANNA ROSE

The concept of "networking" as a way to move ahead professionally is one that has captured the career woman's imagination, perhaps because it agrees with what most of us already secretly suspect: Who you know is as least as important as what you know. While perhaps unfairly cynical, there seems to be some ring of truth to the idea that knowing the right people can help a career. Certainly for a beginning professional, having other people looking out for your interests is likely to be an asset, especially if they are well-established in the field.

WHY BUILD A NETWORK?

The intellectual stimulation a professional network provides is the foremost reason for a scholar to develop one. Colleagues who are willing to review your manuscripts and grants, who will ask your advice about their research, and who will discuss research design and new developments in your field are an invaluable part of the process of scholarly inquiry. The research process is embedded in a social context which involves, not only formal public distribution of research, but also informal communication between colleagues (Reskin, 1978). The ivory tower is a far from lonely place — it is a lively intellectual environment that is national or even international in scope. Your ability to tap into this wellspring of intellectual riches will affect both the quality of your work and your career.

The dependence on informal communication has two other consequences for the scholar, particularly in the sciences. First, having a national network of colleagues in your area will provide you with access to current developments before their formal communication in journals and books (Garvey, 1979). Thus, colleagues are your entry into the preprint network, access to which may determine whether your research is outdated before it's published, or whether it is "on the cutting edge." Second, just as publishing provides opportunities for peer evaluation, informal interaction and circulation of manuscripts does, too. Both help to establish a researcher's reputation and promote her or his visibility within the field.

Having a professional reputation, in turn, provides further opportunities for intellectual stimulation. According to Frieze (1983), there are at least three major advantages of having a "reputation." First, being known in the field provides opportunities for publications not open to the unknown scholar, including being asked to contribute to books, to participate in symposia, to collaborate, and to attend special conferences. A second advantage is that one gains access to inside information in the field by being asked to review manuscripts, being sent unpublished and prepublished papers, and receiving information on federal and foundation funds. Third, once one has developed a professional reputation, one can become a "gatekeeper," helping to define the field by reviewing articles and books, writing tenure and promotion letters, and assuming journal editorship.

In addition to affecting your scholarship, colleagues will have a profound effect on your career at three points (at least): getting your first job (and possibly subsequent ones), during the tenure decision, and during promotion decisions. Through their letters of recommendation and national contacts, faculty-colleagues from your graduate institution will influence your first job placement. How well you have developed your network also will be crucial during tenure and promotion decisions. A carefully developed national network should supply you with candidates to serve as outside evaluators for your tenure and promotion reviews. To be effective, these colleagues should be established scholars and know your work and you personally, if possible. In addition, without allies in your departmental network, you may jeopardize your chances of getting tenure and/or promotion.

Two other important functions professional networks fulfill are helping to socialize the novice and providing a source of friendship. Colleagues "socialize" the new professional by communicating expectations concerning the norms, protocols, ethics, and ideals of the profession (Becker & Strauss, 1956; Terborg, 1977). Advice informally communicated during the socialization process could be information about how to approach certain individuals in your department, how formal criteria are *really* weighted, and the "unwritten" criteria for tenure (see Gibbons' chapter). Networks provide a valuable source of occupationally-based friendships, too. Such friendships both support the individual and increase the social and moral solidarity of the network (Barnard, 1938; Hess, 1972). Friendships with colleagues in your network will solidify your identity as a professional as well as provide you with sympathy and concrete help if you lose or want to leave your present job.

ISSUES FOR WOMEN

Every serious professional should be concerned about developing her or his network. However, research on academicians indicates that women may have more difficulty establishing a network than men, and that even once established, women's networks function less effectively in some areas. According to Epstein (1971), women in male-dominated professions are likely to be excluded from much of the informal interaction of professional life that occurs in social contexts like university clubs, bars, poker games, or athletic clubs.

A personal anecdote from a friend serves to illustrate this point. In the five years she has been at her present institution, not one senior faculty and only one junior faculty member in her department has invited her to his or her home. Whether this is due to her being single and/or a woman is unclear. Regardless, the social environment of her department as she experiences it is quite different from that lived by her two married male junior colleagues, both of whom were "wooed" by various senior faculty when they arrived. Invitations flowed to jog, play raquetball, go to dinner, or go camping. One of the men, a friend of hers, complained about the burden of these obligatory interactions, as he wasn't interested in having his friendship and colleague networks overlap to this degree. Nevertheless, by being offered opportunities for interaction, he was being offered the *choice* to develop those relationships if he so desired, a choice she wasn't offered.

Empirical evidence of women's social exclusion is also available. Finding someone with whom to have lunch or even talk over ideas was cited as a problem for women Ph.D.s studied by Simon, Clark, and Galway (1967). Similarly, women medical students reported being excluded from the informal networks of male students (Kutner & Brogan, 1981). Kaufman (1978) found that women faculty have fewer male colleague friends in their network and fewer higher status associates than male faculty. Women psychologists also have less direct access to high status professionals than men (Denmark, 1980).

In my own research on the professional networks of assistant professors in psychology (Rose, 1985) and biology (unpublished data), women's networks differed from men's in some of the same ways described above. Respondents listed people with whom they had "an important colleague relationship," at the departmental, university, and national level. No sex difference in network size was found, but the composition of women's and men's networks differed significantly in both disciplines. Among psychologists, men had significantly more contacts from their graduate institution and fewer women in their network than women. Among biologists, the sex composition of the network was similar for males and females, but male assistant professors were significantly more likely to be *friends* with higher ranking males than their female junior faculty counterparts.

Women's networks also appear to be less effective than men's in certain areas. Leviton and Whitely (1981) reported that women Ph.D. students were less likely than men to have heard of job offers through announcements to departments, indicating that the women may not have been part of the informal communication network of the department. In my research on psychologists, women reported their networks to be less effective than men's in the area of "helping develop a professional reputation." Women rated their colleagues as significantly less effective than men's at enhancing their professional visibility, as less likely to have recommended their work to other colleagues, and as having expended less effort in helping them establish a network (Rose, 1985).

In conclusion, the research suggests that women's networks may be less adequate at providing some or all of the network functions, including professional visibility, access to information concerning jobs and developments in the field, friendship, and socialization. Consequently, it is particularly important for women to consciously monitor, expand, and nurture their network. There are some healthy signs that women are already doing so. The women psychologists and biologists I reported about earlier had, on the average, at least one higher ranking woman and two women peers in their network. The existence of a small same-sex support network within the larger network may provide support and friendship as well as reduce feelings of isolation. Even so, women may still have problems maintaining ties with colleagues from their graduate institution, establishing friendships with higher ranking men and men peers, and developing a professional reputation.

A FEMINIST PHILOSOPHY OF COLLEGIALITY

The suggestions to be proposed here for how to build a professional network derive from a feminist philosophy concerning the goals and process of developing colleague relationships. In the competitive and hierarchical world of academe and the research community, the emphasis seems to be on "besting" each other and improving one's own status. While women deserve the chance to advance their careers, too, it is possible to do so in a more cooperative and egalitarian manner, thus changing the very nature of the professional environment. It is important to consider what one can give as well as what one can get from a professional network. One has a responsibility to extend one's 'gifts" to those of lower status as well as higher, including sharing expertise, ideas, or praise. A respect for and genuine appreciation of others' strengths and compassion for their shortcomings is also a crucial aspect of collective collegiality.

HOW TO BUILD A NETWORK

Publishing a lot is certainly one way to build a network, but there are other ways for the novice to develop collegial ties without having written the definitive article in the field and produced the research to back it. Though some may start to develop their professional network at the undergraduate level, friends and faculty from graduate school will constitute the first network for most. Hence, developing good relationships with a broad base of faculty and fellow students in graduate school is a good strategy. If properly tended, these connections will help you survive and perhaps thrive while adjusting to the pressures of your first job. For instance, having friends who are willing, somehow, to fit your work on "Medieval Saints" into their symposium on "Women in Contemporary Literature" just might give you the public exposure you need to get started.

Your graduate contacts probably will constitute the core of your national network once you get your first faculty position. Because women's ties with their graduate institution tend to be weaker, you may have to decide whether to do more than your share of the work to maintain them, to develop other national contacts to replace them, or both. Once you begin your job, departmental and university networks should also be established; both will provide invaluable support and information about how the university functions.

There are four basic strategies that can aid you in establishing your national, departmental, and university network: conference presentations, collaboration, correspondence, and 'community" involvement in professional organizations. Each will be described separately.

Conference Presentations

Presenting your work at a professional conference is one of the most useful and enjoyable ways to improve the intellectual quality of your scholarship, publicize your work, and expand your national network. However, conferences are exhausting both personally and financially, so it is important to weigh the potential benefits with the cost. Factors to take into account when planning what conferences to attend include the size and prestige of the conference, the type of audience you want to reach, and the likelihood of your attending the conference regularly.

In general, you will meet more people at small conferences than large ones unless you are active in a division or subcommittee of the association. It's easier to establish an acquaintance at a small conference and renew it at a big one than vice versa. Because of the narrower focus of smaller conferences, common interests are already apparent, easing social interaction. On the other hand, though smaller conferences provide more opportunities for repeated interaction, the large conventions provide exposure to a broader audience.

Presenting a paper or poster session at a conference will provide you with more advantages professionally than will merely attending. Why pass up the chance to discuss your research with other experts? Unless you are from a large department that has many other faculty in your area, it may be one of the few chances available to interact with a group of colleagues that share your interests. It's best to take copies of your paper to the conference with you to distribute. *Be sure to include a citation on the paper* (Frieze, 1983). Countless papers distributed at conventions fail to mention the author, title, conference, or date, making it impossible for anyone to cite that research or contact the author. If it isn't possible for you to bring copies of your paper, be sure to have a sign-up sheet for reprint requests and mail copies of your paper to interested persons soon after the conference.

Another strategy is to organize a symposium or panel. This takes more planning but gives you the opportunity to invite people doing work related to yours. Consider inviting people who are well-established in your area; even if they don't accept, they can suggest other speakers for your program and are likely to be flattered that you asked.

In addition to presenting your work while you're at the conference, it is important to attend conferences with some regularity. Going to one here and there occasionally may be sufficient once you are established, but attending annually is better at the early professional stage. Keep in mind that the amount of time you spend with a new acquaintance may be only 20 minutes at a social hour. It's difficult enough to remember details about the person one year later, much less two or three.

By now you might be getting the impression that professional conferences are serious business. That is precisely the message I'm trying to convey. Going to conventions to spend one day at the sessions then vacationing the rest of the time isn't going to develop your network. Similarly, showing up only for your own session and then leaving will deprive you of valuable opportunities to socialize. Traveling with a spouse or lover who might compete with your attention at the conference can be a disadvantage. It might be best to consider going alone.

Another aspect of going to conferences that can make it more work than play is the stress produced by meeting people, or more precisely, taking the *initiative* in meeting people. (The odds are slim that you are going to meet other people by waiting for them to approach *you*.) Unless (and perhaps even if) you are "well-connected," that is, your dissertation adviser is famed Dr. So-and-So, your dissertation was awarded the Young Researcher Award, or you are at Prestige University, people might not be very friendly. If you are a graduate student or assistant professor, you might find that some people of higher rank will disregard you. Academicians are not exempt from undesirable human traits like snobbery. Of course, there are also other reasons someone might not give you her or his attention, among them being that most people are ill at ease socially when common interests (e.g., mutual friends or research) aren't apparent.

The possibility of being rebuffed and the strain of carrying on a conversation with a stranger keep many women I know carefully ensconced in cliques of old friends, waiting for someone to approach *them*. This need not be the case. Based on my attendance at 10 professional conferences over the past five years, I've developed a set of guidelines to help weather conference ups and downs:

The goal is to find likable colleagues. Basing the quest on liking rather than utility is more compatible with most people's value system. Try to find people with enough in common both academically and interpersonally to warrant developing that connection. It's not necessary to ingratiate yourself to anyone to develop useful connections. There are enough people that are both likable *and* helpful that you do not have to base your search solely on self-interest.

Assume most of the responsibility for both initiating the interaction and maintaining the conversation. This doesn't mean you should do all the talking, only that you will take primary responsibility for drawing the other person out by asking questions. If questions aren't reciprocated (many people don't know what to ask), offer appropriate information about yourself anyway. Assuming this responsibility will give you a sense of control over your fate — you haven't made the error of expecting more from a stranger than she or he can contribute.

Rebuffs will happen. Try not to take these personally. I usually monitor my mood each day to determine how many rebuffs my ego can stand. Then I make a bargain with myself that I won't get upset or paranoid until after I meet with my Xth rejection, whereupon I'll hide out someplace for a while.

Nothing risked, nothing gained. It might be a lot more comfortable to go to dinner with people you already know, but you may lose the opportunity to establish a rapport with some new people that comes only by socializing together.

Enjoy old friends. Maintaining old ties is clearly another reason to attend conferences. It's also fun. If possible, try to introduce old and new colleagues to each other and create new social groups.

In summary, professional conferences provide unparalleled opportunities for intellectual stimulation and social interaction. Once you've established a hearty core of graduate school friends and new acquaintances, the convention pace becomes exhilarating and rewarding.

Collaboration

Collaboration is a second means of developing a professional network. Consider collaborating with graduate students as well as colleagues on research or editorial projects. Even if comprised of only two people, the sense of being part of an "enterprise" may enhance your professional identity as well as provide motivation, stimulation, and continuity to your work. Collaborators are also a source of knowledge concerning departmental or national politics and a potential friendship pool. (Also see chapter by Stake.)

Correspondence

Corresponding with colleagues nationally is a good way to build your network. Graduate school is the time to start. Write to people whose research interests are similar to yours, describing your research and asking to be placed on their reprint list. It is wise to expand your professional correspondence at the junior faculty level, particularly since women's networks seem to function less effectively in helping develop a professional reputation. Frieze (1983) has suggested sending copies of your papers to well-known others even if they haven't been requested, and recommends sending related papers (or a list of related papers) when asked for reprints. In addition, if you met someone at a conference, follow-up that contact with a letter.

Community

Developing a network through community refers to getting active in professional groups and organizations. More of your strengths are likely to be revealed to people that have worked with you than to those who know your research only from your published work. Attending and organizing informal seminars and conferences is one way to develop your own "community." By providing this service to your department, for instance, you will meet new people and be responsible for enhancing your colleagues' intellectual development.

One woman I know, a junior faculty member at a major university, met every major researcher in her field during her second year by agreeing to coordinate speakers for a graduate class. The visiting faculty were invited for two-week periods; she selected the speakers and acted as host to each. Not only did they all get to know her fairly well, but two years later she had a grant funded to work with one person she had met during the visit.

Becoming active in professional communities outside your own field is also very beneficial for women. As mentioned in the Rohrbaugh chapter, Women's Studies Programs or feminist political groups provide a source of support untainted by the anxieties and jealousies that sometimes plague relationships with colleagues with whom one is competing. My involvement in a feminist study group over the past several years has been one such refuge, supplying both political challenges and much needed validation for my identity as a feminist and academic. In addition, my Women's Studies network has provided precious advice, inside information, and support that has been useful to me professionally and personally.

To become part of a professional community at the national level, a useful strategy is to get involved in a subcommittee or division of an association. (See the Appendix for a list of relevant professional organizations.) Most organizations are looking for workers and it's easy to gain entry by attending business meetings or volunteering for some task. The Task Force on Strategies for Getting and Keeping a Job that produced this manual is an example of the effectiveness of this type of networking. Few of the committee members knew each other before; the project enabled us to collaborate on the content, develop our own ideas in individual chapters, learn from each other, present a symposium at the American Psychological Association, get to know other members of the sponsor division (Psychology of Women), and produce an exciting and worthwhile product.

CONCLUSION

Once you have established your network, your responsibility to yourself and others has not ended. Try to draw other women into it and participate in their professional development by collaborating, corresponding, and cooperating with them on research and projects which will help others. Perhaps most important, don't forget to praise other women (Hartmann, 1983). Women may not get much recognition from male colleagues and are generally less inclined than men to brag about themselves. We must do this for each other, commending a woman directly for teaching a successful course, doing good scholarship, or making other contributions, in addition to praising her to male colleagues, nonfeminist women, and students. Women with tenure or full rank will continue to need this encouragement; don't assume that because she has "made it," she no longer needs support. If she is doing her job as a feminist, she will continue to feel marginal and alienated in the university and will benefit from your praise. Last, you should never hear a favorable comment about a female colleague without passing it on to her (Hartmann, 1983). If we work together, we can live more easily in the male-dominated university.

REFERENCES

Barnard, C. (1938). The functions of the executive. Cambridge: Harvard University Press.

Becker, H.S., & Strauss, A.L. (1956). Careers, personality, and adult socialization. *American Journal of Sociology, 62,* 253–263.

Denmark, F.L. (1980). Psyche: From rocking the cradle to rocking the boat. *American Psychologist, 35*(12), 1057–1065.

Epstein, C.F. (1971). *Woman's place.* Berkeley: University of California Press.

Frieze, I.H. (1983, June). *Developing a professional reputation.* Paper presented at the National Women's Studies Association, Columbus, OH.

Garvey, W.D. (1979). *Communication: The essence of science.* New York: Pergamon Press.

Hartmann, S. (1983, June). *Survival strategies for feminists in academe.* Paper presented at the National Women's Studies Association, Columbus, OH.

Hess, E. (1972). Friendship. In M.W. Riley, M. Johnson, & A. Foner (Eds.), *Aging and society.* (Vol. 3, pp. 357–393). New York: Russell Sage.

Kaufman, D.R. (1978). Associational ties in academe: Some male and female differences. *Sex Roles, 4*(1), 9–21.

Kutner, N.B., & Brogan, D.R. (1981). Problems of colleagueship for women entering the medical profession. *Sex Roles, 7*(7), 739–746.

Leviton, L.C., & Whitely, S.E. (1981). Job seeking patterns of female and male Ph.D. recipients. *Psychology of Women Quarterly, 5*(5), 690–701.

Reskin, B.F. (1978). Sex differentiation and the social organization of science. *Sociological Inquiry, 48,* 6–37.

Rose, S.M. (1985). Professional networks of junior faculty in psychology. *Psychology of Women Quarterly, 9*(4), 533-547.

Simon, R.J., Clark, S.M., & Galway, S. (1967). The woman Ph.D.: A recent profile. *Social Problems, 15,* 221–236.

Terborg, J.R. (1977). Women in management: A research review. *Journal of Applied Psychology, 62*(6), 647–664.

■ 5
When It's Publish or Perish: Tips on Survival

JAYNE E. STAKE

If you land a job in academia and you are on a "tenure track," then you know that keeping your job is contingent on satisfying certain expectations that go with your position. It is important to determine as soon as possible what those expectations are. Once you learn how much you must publish to be granted tenure, you have a decision to make. If you decide that the expectations are unreasonable or higher than your interest in fulfilling them, then you will want to consider a game plan for making a job transition sometime before your tenure decision year. A number of chapters in this book provide advice on developing such a plan. If, on the other hand, you decide that you want to work for tenure, and if your tenure decision will be based partially on original scholarly activity, then you must become successful in getting your work published. The purpose of this chapter is to provide some advice for those who want to learn to publish and not to "perish."

The road to publication is different for journal manuscripts than for book manuscripts. Because most young scholars earn their tenure through journal publications, this article is directed primarily to the process of journal publication. However, some ideas for finding a book publisher will be provided later in this chapter. Additional suggestions concerning how to publish can be found in *Productive Scholarship: Issues, Problems, Solutions*, (Fox, 1985).

Getting your work published in scholarly journals can be a difficult and frustrating process. I myself experienced considerable anxiety and distress in learning how to survive the publication process, and I have spoken with a number of other women who have had experiences very similar to mine. After considering this problem for a number of years, I've come to the conclusion that it is almost inevitable that young Ph.D.s beginning their careers will have some difficulty in adjusting to the publication process. One problem is that all of us who have earned a doctorate and who have been successful in landing an academic job have a long history of success at academic endeavors. We are accustomed to receiving straight A's and to being singled out by teachers as being particularly bright students. Our scholarly activities have brought us recognition and praise, and we are, therefore, not prepared for major criticism and rejection of our work.

When you submit your work to an editor for publication, however, you are in a very different situation than when you were a student. Your work is no longer being compared to that of other students and you are no longer being judged by teachers, who are likely to be encouraging in their judgments of your work. Instead, you are compared to others in your field, most of whom will be more experienced than you. Anonymous reviewers will judge your manuscript, and they may not take the time or care to be encouraging or constructive in their criticisms of your work. Furthermore, in submitting your work to a journal you are competing with others for very limited space; many journals accept less than 20 % of the manuscripts they receive. Hence, the odds are very high that at least some of your work will be rejected by editors. This is quite different from the educational situation you have been used to in which all or most of your work was accepted and rewarded.

The first step in learning to survive the publication process is, therefore, to learn to accept criticism and rejection of your work. Probably the most critical time in a young researcher's academic life is when those first rejections arrive in the mail. Your emotional, cognitive, and behavioral reactions to those rejections will determine to a large extent whether you survive the tenure process. A number of women have told me that when they received a rejection, they filed their manuscript away with a vague notion that they would return to it later and would try to get their work published elsewhere. Time slipped by and the paper was never published. As they reduced their scholarly efforts, they lost faith in their own competence. This is a vicious cycle. The less time and energy you devote to research, the less likely you are to experience success in getting your work published and the less likely you are to maintain confidence in your ability as a scholar and researcher.

STRATEGIES FOR PUBLISHING

You can avoid the vicious cycle described above by developing an objective, nonpersonal attitude toward the journal publication process. Following are some tips for using the process to your best advantage.

Thoroughly research the journals in your content area to determine the journal that is most appropriate for your paper. Sending your paper to an inappropriate journal can only lengthen the time it takes to get your work published and result in an unnecessary rejection. To determine the journals most likely to be receptive to your work, read the instructions to authors provided by the journals and look through recent issues of journals to find out which topic areas, research methods, and styles of presentation are in each.

Of all the journals that might accept your paper, send yours to the most prestigious. Although you have the greatest chance of rejection from the "better" journals, you are likely to get better quality criticism from the journals with more stringent criteria for acceptance. Also, if your paper is accepted in a better quality journal, your work will tend to be evaluated more positively at the time of your tenure decision.

Another criterion you may want to consider when you choose your journals is the average length of the journal's review process and the publication lag (i.e., how long it will take for your article to be published once it's accepted). If possible, select those journals that promise a shorter (e.g. three-month) turnaround time for the review process and that do not have a large publication backlog.

An additional consideration in selecting a journal is the type of people who read it. Before deciding on a publication outlet, think about the audience you would like to reach. Who will be most interested in your research? How will your ideas have the most impact? Who can most benefit from your ideas? Once you have decided on your audience, keep them in mind as you write your article. An article may be written in more technical terms for some audiences than for others. Be sure that the level and tone of your article is appropriate to the audience you have chosen.

Develop a contingency plan for getting your paper published. Have at least one alternate journal in mind for your manuscript in case it is not accepted by the first journal you send it to. It's a good idea to expect that your paper may be rejected when first sent for review. Think of this first review as an opportunity to receive comments from experts in your field. These comments will help you to improve your manuscript and may lead to better quality research in your future work. Given this outlook, critical comments from reviewers and editors can be seen as a useful and necessary part of the publication process, rather than as painful rejections.

When you receive feedback from an editor, read it carefully to determine the disposition of the manuscript. Editors and reviewers classify manuscripts into four broad categories: (1) acceptance of manuscript as is (a very rare event); (2) acceptance pending certain specified revisions; (3) rejection with suggestions for resubmission; and (4) absolute rejection.

By reading the letter from the editor and the written comments of reviewers, you will be able to determine which of the four categories fits your paper. Once you know this and once you understand what the criticisms of the reviewers are, you must decide what you're going to do with your paper. Here are some guidelines:

1. If the editor has agreed to accept your paper pending specified changes, then by all means go ahead with those changes. Once an editor has agreed to accept your paper, then you can be quite certain that you will have your work published. Be sure to keep any correspondence from the editor to ensure that you have a record of the editor's agreement to publish.

Whenever you decide to resubmit a paper to an editor, it's a good idea to notify the editor immediately of your intention to revise your paper and the date you expect to resubmit it. Then make it a top priority to keep your own deadline. When you resubmit your paper, include a detailed list of the revisions you made. Be sure the list makes reference to all of the criticisms addressed by the reviewers. If you believe that one or more of the criticisms was invalid, indicate in your letter to the editor why you think so. Do not make a change in your manuscript that you think will weaken it. Instead, explain why you decided not to make the suggested changes.

2. If the editor has rejected the paper but asked for a resubmission, you still have a good chance of eventually having your paper accepted. Read what the editor and reviewers have said about needed changes. If you do not think you can make those changes, or if you do not want to

make any additional effort on your paper, you can send it to the next journal on your list. Think carefully about this decision, however. If you have an opportunity to improve your manuscript and to have it appear in a "better" journal, it is almost always worth the extra effort to make the changes necessary. Your reputation as a researcher will depend upon what you eventually have in print, so it's an excellent investment of time and effort to revise your manuscript in line with the suggestions of experts in your field. Also, the visibility of your work will depend, in part, on *where* it appears, and you will be judged for tenure partially on the basis of *where* your work is published.

3. If the editor has rejected the paper and has not asked for a revision, it is best not to plan a resubmission of the paper to the same editor. Instead, look over your paper to see how you may improve it for another journal. The first set of reviewers will probably have provided you with some suggestions or criticisms that can guide a revision of the work. The comments of these reviewers can lead to an improved version of your paper that may have a better chance for acceptance by the next journal on your list.

4. In reviewing your work following a rejection it may be that you will determine that the paper cannot be "saved" by a revision. Perhaps the basic premise or research design was faulty. It is certainly normal to be discouraged at this point. Yet this is still a time to be active in working toward your publication goal.

You must first diagnose what you think the problem is. If you believe the rationale for the study was weak or misguided, do some more reading, thinking on your own, and/or talking with colleagues to help you in reconceptualizing the problem. If you are in the social or natural sciences and you are having trouble with research design or statistics, seek the advice of colleagues, review your statistics notes and texts from previous classwork, or consider the possibility of additional formal training to help you at this time.

Whatever you decide, do not give up on yourself simply because you have not been successful in this attempt to have your work published. Remember that even this experience is worthwhile because it has provided you with information that will be helpful to your eventual success as a researcher.

The above suggestions apply primarily to journal publication. The means of finding a book publisher are somewhat different, requiring different strategies. Before deciding to write a book, you should first consider carefully whether it's a good idea to be writing books before tenure. In some disciplines and in some departments such efforts will be well rewarded. In others, they will not. So first determine how much a successful book publication will "count" toward your tenure decision.

If you decide that you do want to write a book, there are several ways to find a publisher. You may write a letter to a variety of publishers describing your idea, and asking whether they have an interest in your topic. If an editor expresses interest, you can follow up with more information about the book, including a table of contents and sample chapters.

Another way to make contact with editors is to write to them shortly before you plan to attend a conference in your area of interest. You can indicate in your letter that you would like to meet during the convention to discuss the possibility of publishing with their company.

A third way to find a publisher is to talk with the book sales representatives with whom you come in contact to discuss your own needs for books. The better salespeople know what their companies are interested in and what needs their company has for new books. In fact, in talking with book sales representatives about your needs for a text, you may find them asking you if you have an interest in writing for them.

The final way to find a publisher is to first publish one or more articles in journals. Book publishers who are interested in finding scholars in your field may approach you once you have shown yourself to be a published expert.

PRETENURE ADVICE

There are a few other, more general pieces of advice for you to consider as you plan your pretenure years.

Timing. People in tenure-track positions have limited time to satisfy tenure requirements, yet the time between completion of a manuscript and its acceptance to a journal is quite lengthy. It can take six months to a year to receive feedback on your manuscript from the first review. If your paper needs revising, and especially if you must send the paper to a second or third editor, it will be an extended time period before your completed manuscript is eventually accepted. Given the limited time period for proving yourself as a researcher, and given high expectations for publication, it is important to begin your research program when you first enter your position and the tenure clock begins to tick. To delay a year or two before getting started could mean the difference between a positive and negative tenure decision.

Remedy weaknesses. If you have received feedback from teachers, editors, or reviewers that indicates that you have deficits in your writing skills, work to improve them early in your career. Depending on the problem, it may be helpful to enroll in an extension writing course, to seek advice from those you know who are good writers, and/or to read a general guide to grammar and composition. Furthermore, it's important for you to proofread your own work very carefully. Once you have completed a first draft of your manuscript, put it away for a few days. Then go back to it to get a fresh perspective. You will probably find that you can improve your own manuscript substantially by taking a second, objective look at it.

Do not "put all your research eggs in one basket." Plan a research program that does not hinge on your having success with one particular theoretical idea or one particular research project. It is better, for example, not to plan extensive longitudinal studies during your first years as a researcher, for then you are dependent on a particular group of subjects for your survival. Let me give you an example. I know a researcher who planned an elaborate two-year longitudinal study of laboratory animals. All of the researcher's time and energy was devoted to this study for more than one year. There was a power failure in the building, which eventually resulted in the death of all the animals. Even humans, who are certainly heartier subjects, have a way of being difficult to follow over time. Thus, although you may very much want to conduct a longitudinal study to address your research problem, it's probably best to postpone those more ambitious projects until after the tenure decision.

If you can't resist launching into a long-range project, think about ways you can produce some short-range "products" from your work along the way. For example, you may be able to publish a paper about your longitudinal subjects based upon initial data collection. Or you may be able to produce a short essay based upon an initial section of your full-length book.

Utilize colleagues. The advice of your colleagues can be particularly helpful during your first research years. Colleagues can offer emotional support, advice about your research, and advice specific to your department. Elsewhere in this book is more detailed information about the value of professional mentors and networks (chapters by Rose and by Barnes).

Colleagues may also collaborate with you on joint research projects. The main advantages of collaboration are (1) The opportunity to learn directly about the research process from colleagues, particularly the "nuts and bolts" of carrying through on research initiatives; (2) The intellectual stimulation of working on a research team rather than in isolation; and (3) The increased number of publications possible when you are combining your efforts with others.

However, there are some disadvantages to consider as well: (1) If your are collaborating with a more senior researcher, you may not be given the credit due to you for your research efforts. The research may be credited primarily to your more senior colleague, even though you may have done much of it yourself with little guidance from your colleague. For gaining tenure it is usually necessary to demonstrate that you can work independently. (2) When you collaborate with others you become dependent upon them to carry out their responsibilities to the project. If they slow down or back out of their participation in the project, you will be left "holding the bag." Hence, it's important to be very careful in selecting only those colleagues you can fully trust to carry out their part of the project, particularly if you do not feel you could carry on independently with the project.

Don't delay writing. Some young scholars have many valuable ideas and pursue worthwhile research projects but fail to sit themselves down to do the writing necessary to produce publishable manuscripts. There are a number of reasons why manuscripts don't get written, including a dislike of the solitary writing process and a fear that the manuscript, once written, will be rejected. If you find that you are not getting down to the business of writing on a regular basis, then analyze what the problem is for you and develop strategies to ensure that you do get your necessary writing done. The chapter by Rogers in this book provides some suggestions and references that you can use to develop a successful writing pattern.

Persist. One of the single most important attributes of the researcher is persistence. Of all the researchers who have received tenure in institutions that stressed publication of scholarly work, every one of them persisted in their work, and for all of them you can be sure that there were times when things did not go smoothly. Sometimes equipment failed, data did not confirm predictions, writing was difficult, and editors failed to see the value of their work. It was only through persistence that they were eventually successful in their goal to publish their research.

There are many obstacles in the way of your finding the answers to your research questions and of your presenting your ideas in published form, but these challenges are part of what makes the work of a scholar an intriguing and satisfying process. Once you have begun to publish your research, you will find a number of satisfactions, in addition to a secure academic position. Because your papers are in print, others will have an opportunity to learn and benefit from your work. Some will write to you for further information and will be influenced by your work in planning their own research. You may be called upon to contribute to a journal or edited volume in your field, or to speak nationally or locally on your field of expertise. You will also be asked to serve as a journal reviewer yourself, and will therefore have an opportunity to provide guidance to others who are working in your field.

REFERENCE

Fox, M.F. (Ed.). (1985). *Productive scholarship: Issues, problems, solutions.* Boulder, CO: Westview Press.

◼ 6
Transitions and Stresses for Black Female Scholars

DENISE R. BARNES

Optimally, a Black woman enters the university system with a host of potentially rewarding experiences available to her. Accessibility to these experiences will depend on a combination of her own personal style and capabilities and the character of her department and university. One Black woman might enter the system with a clear, well-founded belief that this parochial, chauvinistic, traditional system has worked hard to keep her out or to limit her involvement and advancement. Another might come without such preconceived notions and learn to maneuver the uncertain academic course by trial and error. Both will have come with the ability and desire to engage in scholarly work and to become successful. However, as they try to keep one step ahead of the tenure clock, Black female scholars may be derailed by discriminatory practices and attitudes of the administration, colleagues, and students.

In this chapter, the intent is to identify the transitions and associated stresses Black women faculty face as they enter white academic institutions. Four types of transitions (Schlossberg, 1984) will be addressed: anticipated transitions, unanticipated transitions, chronic "hassles," and nonevents.

ANTICIPATED TRANSITIONS

Anticipated transitions are ones which are expected based on newly assumed roles or normative life-cycle events. Like others in academe, Black women faculty expect to engage in research, teach, and offer their services to the university and the community at large. Most Black women understand the demands of the job; they know they must produce to gain tenure. What is complicated, though, is determining nuances regarding the weights given to various criteria for tenure. A Black woman knows she must publish, but the standards for excellence and scholarly works are vague. Does she work to satisfy her own scientific curiosity or does she publish to satisfy the idiosyncracies of her particular department or university? How should she present herself as a scholar and a unique individual? Black women probably have not had much guidance concerning these issues.

While the anticipated transition from graduate student to assistant professor is difficult for most new faculty, Black female scholars must face it without guidance and support from those who have gone through similar pressures before them. A strategy which can be used to cope with anticipated transitions is to seek out a mentor. Since there are few Black women in academe, it may not be possible to find a Black woman mentor. It may be necessary to search outside the department or discipline or even university to find a suitable candidate, Black or white. It is best to engage someone who is sensitive to the Black woman scholar's plight, but who is also intellectually demanding.

Uncertainty about her new role makes it important for a Black woman to have a strong sense of what constitutes her identity. However, she must also be flexible, enthusiastic, and receptive to constructive criticism. She should accept the mistakes she makes and work to rectify them. She also needs to develop her own criteria for success. One woman spoke of her confusion when she got wind of her colleagues being more concerned about how she dressed (she wore conservative dresses and suits while most of the males in her department wore jeans) than in her scholarly work. She expected her colleagues to consider her as a serious academic and not concern themselves with fashion. She ignored the rumblings about her attire and continued to maintain her academic productivity. Recognizing that what worked for others in her department could have been personally disastrous for her, she avoided being imitative. An internal standard of success helped her to ignore this petty distraction and concentrate on her professional strengths.

UNANTICIPATED TRANSITIONS

Unanticipated transitions are not predictable; they have little or no relationship to normative life-cycle transitions (Schlossberg, 1984). Occupational events which could be labeled unanticipated include being fired or demoted, giving up work because of illness, or leaving a job for a better one (Pearlin, 1980). The inherent lack of anticipatory socialization makes it difficult to prepare for these events.

Because Black female scholars have few role-models, many stresses of new faculty members are unanticipated. For example, since Black women are relative novices in the academic arena, they tend not to request information or bargain for services usually offered to whites (assistance with housing, moving fees, research space, optimum salary for her level of experience). Their transition into the world of work becomes difficult and sensitivity is heightened when they discover how their colleagues are treated both socially and professionally. Many do not know that it is quite appropriate to get to know their deans, chairperson, and division heads on many levels. These administrators know that she is a member of the faculty, but depending on their interest and size of the institution, a Black female may only be a statistic and not known with respect to her area of expertise. It is useful to have lunch with some of these administrators to fill them in.

Accepting an academic position also results in some unanticipated transitions regarding the Black woman Ph.D.'s relationship with the Black community. Many Black women scholars have found it frustrating to realize that people in their communities do not know what they do. Publishing and producing is an invisible job and is not characteristic of the traditional types of jobs held by workers in the Black community (e.g. salesperson, day-care worker, mail carrier, police officer, domestic, elementary and high school teacher). For example, one colleague complained that although she had explained her position several times to her 55-year-old aunt, the aunt, in satisfying inquires about her niece, would offer, "She's still going to State University and I think she's teaching too!" Some women have used their expertise to give talks at local churches and sororities in order to become a resource for the community. In some respects they "actualize" their professional identity to the community at large.

An additional problem is that most parents of Black female scholars have worked within the Black community in jobs which did not require that Blacks and whites work as colleagues in an ostensibly egalitarian environment. In response to an item in a pilot study by this author on Black middle-aged daughters and their mothers, a respondent wrote:

> When I was at the University and grumbling to my parents about the tensions of the work place and racial politics in particular, my mother observed that her generation had it easier than mine in that aspect. She said that they knew the rules of segregation, and it was pretty much keep out of the way of white folks. But our generation works in a time when racial mores are not only shifting, but they differ from place to place. My mother says we never know what to expect or know for sure what's expected of us socially from whites.
>
> Even women younger than I who grew up in the South would have come up under segregation — segregated schools and probably segregated colleges. But our generation, if professional, must work in mostly white settings, with few exceptions. What does that do to one's assumptions about control of the environment from without or within?

Most Black women scholars expect that they will be confronted with racist attitudes and practices somewhere along the academic road. They will be unfamiliar with how these practices and attitudes will manifest themselves. Many have internalized the negative feelings they have gotten from interactions with colleagues and have left academe. Others blame themselves for "letting their guard down," for believing that "we're all in this for the sake of science and intellectual pursuit and nothing else." A few women who had not been promoted felt angry because they had strayed away from the safeguarding behavior of "get it in writing." This practice has been used by many Blacks to maintain privileges that are taken for granted by other groups. Getting it in writing is one coping mechanism that academic practices and policies vigorously avoid.

Black women entering academe learn to recognize that thoughtless and deliberate actions that cause pain and anger are inevitable. White women, as well as white men, may be the source of some of these actions. One Black woman described her feelings of isolation resulting from a social event at her home:

> I was the only Black woman to attend this small interdepartmental women's

group where members would prepare food and meet at each others' homes on a rotating basis. When I invited the group over to my house, there was a noticeable difference in the quality and quantity of food shared and many questions about whether or not I owned my house. I felt funny about continuing my involvement with the group after that. I didn't expect them to be like that. I expected them to make the same positive assumptions about me that I made about them.

To maintain the status quo, colleagues will want Black women faculty to keep their anger under wraps. However, Black women do not need to immediately accept responsibility for insensitive remarks and actions directed to them. One example of this insensitivity occurred to a Black woman who was invited to a parted hosted by a senior colleague. While everyone was circling the table putting food on their plates, he called out to her from the other side, "Oh, don't be so niggardly! You do know what that means, don't you?" She observed that the other people around the table looked a bit puzzled and embarrassed. Her initial impulse was to throw her food at him but she decided to be dignified and stated that she wanted to save room for the dessert. Everyone looked relieved. Later several of her white colleagues apologized for the host's behavior. Such insults to the Black woman's intelligence and sensitivity are not uncommon.

CHRONIC HASSLES

Chronic hassles are a major cause of stress for Black female scholars, and they are derived from any different sources. Leggon (1975) argued that the status hierarchy based on ascribed status (race, sex) is more important in determining professional identity for Black female professionals than achieved status (doctor, professor). Her subjects reported that ascribed status of race was as disadvantageous as the ascribed status of sex. Consequently, it was difficult for some women to distinguish the reasons for why they were being discriminated against.

Epstein (1973) calls this the "double bind," in which Black professionals are caught between the sharp discriminatory cutting edges of racism and sexism. Because Black women scholars cannot readily change either their sex or their race, these two characteristics are the basis for many chronic hassles they experience. One women scholar put it this way:

There's always something. If it's not my colleagues, then it's my students.

For example, one young woman came to my office looking for Dr. ____.
My name was on the door and I was sitting at my desk. She took a brief
look at me, decided I was not the person she wanted, and inquired where
Dr. ____ could be found. When I told her I was Dr. ____, without bat-
ting an eye she immediately asked, "Well, Mrs. ____, I was wondering if
there were still seats available in your 9:30 class?"

This anecdote supports Leggon's findings that ascribed status is more
powerful than achieved status. However, the Black woman must chose
when to fight this bias. She must recognize that every issue is not worth
fighting for. Many times she must ignore small or annoying issues because
she simply does not have the time or energy to respond otherwise. She
must come to terms with what she will compromise (e.g., parking spaces,
office size and location) and what is an absolute must for furthering her
career (e.g., equipment, investigating areas of interest from a different
perspective). She must learn to be a good listener. Colleagues will present
their biases in a host of ways. Some will "forget" to inform her of meetings. Others will assume that she may not have a particular reference or
would not be interested in or have knowledge of their academic area.
Black women should call these possible misconceptions to their colleagues'
attention by being assertive but not aggressive. The absorption rate of
information decreases dramatically when people are on the defensive.
Black women should not allow their colleagues to make them feel guilty
for having these demands.

Some departments have their "token Black" and are not particularly
interested in recruiting or maintaining others. Hence, projecting the image of "super scholar" is unproductive for both the woman and the department. She will lose sight of realistic goals if she tries to do too many things
at once. It is not adaptive for a Black female academic to break her back
to maintain a job that may also be held by mediocre white scholars.

Other chronic hassles will arise around the question of "What is scholarly work?" Intellectual racism assumes that topics like chemistry and
statistics are "pure," "white," and scholarly, and disciplines like Afro-
American studies and social work are not. Many Black women have con-
fessed that they feel anxious about positions in the latter disciplines because of their relatively tenuous stability within the university system.
That is, when "Black is not in" their positions are out. Further, administrators shout with glee when they discover a Black woman with expertise in something other than the "traditionally Black area." Yet these same
administrators have requested that Black female scholars serve as mother/

counselor to Black students, give the "minority opinion" in committees, and offer opinions about the merits of the Afro-American department even if the woman was hired in the chemistry department! These extra duties are never discussed in the negotiations for hiring.

The Black woman academic must learn to say "no." One of the most difficult lessons to learn is to put herself first. Feeling that she is always being scrutinized does not mean that she has to be a "yes person" to survive. She will not be taken seriously if she accepts every challenge, big or small. Activities for which her contributions will be recognized should be pursued. She should do things she enjoys doing without neglecting her intellectual/scholarly requirements. She must guard her time and energy. Black students will make demands and the administration will make demands on behalf of the Black students. Black women scholars have the prerogative to say "no" and risk the label of being "selfish" and "withdrawn." It would be useful to find out how important certain activities are with regard to maintaining a job before a commitment is made.

Most Black female scholars report that they would like to blend their professional work with discovering something about the Black community, whether it be the relationship between Type A personalities (aggressive, prone to cardiac arrests, impatient) and hypertension in Blacks or tracing the history of the relationship between Blacks and Jews in this country. To stay within the guidelines of scholarly pursuit is tricky, because the people who judge our work may decide that it is not worth our time as academics, or that it is not relevant, or that it does not add substantially to the existing literature (which they may or may not know).

This conflict is a real frustration for the Black woman who, like the rest of her colleagues, would like to be able to enjoy and be invested in what she does. Some women have reported that they have worked to discover "what sells" in their departments, worked to complete those requirements and then went on to use the same type of rigor for what they are really interested in doing. Others have "bucked the system" and worked solely with issues regarding Blacks. Some women have survived the rigors of intellectual scrutiny, others have met a more tragic fate. Most women have observed that administrators fail to let them know when anything is wrong. They typically find out at the time of judgment— renewal, promotion, or tenure. In essence, academics is risky business for all involved but it gets riskier when your area of interest is different from the norm.

The term "affirmative action" has clouded the relationship between the hiring of a Black woman and the merits behind that decision. Banks (1984) writes:

> No matter what can be argued about affirmative action as a cause of white resentment and hostility toward Black and women scholars, it is pointless to deny or even minimize the anxiety felt by many minority and women academics who face subtle stigmatization. Scholars, after all, live in a world where cultural assumptions about the mental abilities of Blacks and women are pervasive, assumptions not limited to the academic world. Within the university, a variety of incidents transpires daily that may cause one to reflect on the group, as well as on the origins of one's own experience. (p. 334)

Black women are particularly "suspect" as scholars because of prejudices against affirmative action. Black women are known as "two-fers." That is, two statistical requirements (female and minority) are fulfilled for the price of one. Many Black women are not prepared for the harsh scrutiny of their accomplishments by both male and female colleagues. Painter (1981), a Black woman, recognized the dismay a jobless white male Ph.D. experienced over her having an academic job and put it in the proper perspective:

> I never questioned the justice of my position. I should have a job, and a good one. I had worked hard as a graduate student and had written a decent dissertation. I knew foreign languages, had traveled widely and had taught and published. I thought I had been hired because I was a promising young historian. Unlike the man beside me, I didn't think my teaching at a first-rate university required an extraordinary explanation. (p. 22)

To dispel colleagues' notions that they lack scholarly expertise, Black women faculty need to develop relationships with them at all levels within the department. We can offer to collaborate on projects to display breadth of knowledge, let senior faculty members know our interests and solicit their input, and offer to read, critique, and discuss colleagues' manuscripts.

To counter the chronic hassle of having one's abilities continually questioned, it is useful for a Black women in academia to review her accomplishments time and again in order to minimize the discriminatory attitudes of colleagues who believe she is not skilled enough to be a part of a particular faculty. She should also take a good look at the productivity and skills of other faculty members. Such a review can often be enlightening about how much incompetence the academic community allows when it sees fit.

NONEVENT TRANSITIONS

Nonevent transitions are those for which a person has prepared, but which never come to fruition. The most common nonevent for academics is the failure to secure renewal, promotion, and tenure. The Black female scholar has this stress in common with her colleagues. However, Black women have a relatively poor track record when it comes to hiring and promotion. It is imperative, because of the relative instability of her position, for a Black female scholar to look to the future. She may chose to leave a position for a variety of reasons (e.g., racism, sexism, not enough money), and tenure is never guaranteed.

Part of the reality of self-preservation is diversification. While a high level of academic productivity is important, the Black woman must also make contacts at other universities and outside the academic arena. She can offer workshops to local businesses and community centers to get herself known. She should find out who might be writing grants at local medical centers or nonprofit agencies and determine whether they have a need in her area of expertise. She should seek out consultative relationships and gain skills that are sought after by employers other than universities.

Black women scholars have identified a nonevent that they do not share with their white colleagues. This nonevent is the pervasive feeling that no matter what they do, they will not be seen as a "real" part of their departments or universities. They feel as though they have very little control over how they will be judged. It is important not to let this racism influence one's scholarly productivity or to be continually perched and ready for the next unfair decision from the university or the next racist insult from a colleague. To be a survivor in academe, Black women must learn to reward themselves for their competence and not to internalize negative experiences.

SURVIVING THE TRANSITION

In addition to being isolated from both white female and white male faculty, Black women will find few other Black academics with whom to socialize or collaborate. One way to combat this isolation is to refuse to be alone. Develop relationships outside your department to share concerns and to determine whether other Black academic women have the same experience. Joining the on-campus association of women faculty and/or Black faculty for support and validation is helpful.

Developing a support system outside the academic community is also essential for Black women. The academic community is very close-knit and incestuous. In white circles, academics marry academics or at least their educational equals. The same pattern is evident in social settings. A Black woman cannot afford to get caught in such constraints because her social sphere will be highly diminished. Some women report that they cope with the isolation by sponsoring potluck dinners or house parties (where both males and females contribute) in order to establish relationships with both professional and nonprofessional Blacks. Joining a community church, a carpool, or a sorority can help satisfy personal needs that are not met through work. Also, the benefits of having a housemate as a sounding board outweigh the advantage of having complete privacy. When considering potential mates, Black female scholars are having to broaden their scope. The Black community does not offer substantial numbers of men with comparable academic standing. Some women have rectified this discrepancy by marrying white men.

Because of their relatively scant history as academics in predominantly white institutions, Black female scholars are typically concentrated in the lower tenure-track ranks, in nontenure positions, or in adjunct positions. While a Black woman will probably be pleased with attaining an academic job, many times she has not taken a careful, calculated look at the width and breadth of her position. For example, to be hired by two departments can mean trouble come renewal, promotion, and tenure time. Neither department may want to claim her to sponsor her advancement. Such a position might seem prestigious and "safe" to the novice, but its security is questionable. Some women have turned down interdepartmental positions for that reason or demanded and obtained positions in one department.

Adjunct positions are popular with institutions because they help to satisfy standards for hiring women and Blacks. Although adjunct positions do bring in extra income, the position pays relatively lower wages for doing the same things required for full-time faculty. By virtue of her position, the Black woman adjunct's involvement with students and other faculty members is limited. She has no real power or position to make much of an impact on the university system. A Black woman adjunct should get a clear description of her duties and negotiate responsibilities that seem unreasonable, keeping a close eye on how invested she gets in the work when compensation is inadequate. Administrators are likely to balk when she asks for more salary and involvement in the department. However, keeping a record of her accomplishments and sharing those with a department chairperson or dean sometimes can open up avenues for advancement. (For further tips on adjunct appointments, see chapter by Shepela.)

Black women also might experience lower pay, slower promotion, and higher teaching loads than Black male, white male, and white female scholars (Moore & Wagstaff, 1974). Having the responsibility for larger classes might jeopardize their ability to meet the rigid publishing criteria for tenure. Black women faculty need to bring such discrepancies to the attention of responsible administrators. She should take advantage of leaves of absence in order to enhance her research program. She should maximize the responsibility given to graduate students for computer and library work.

CONCLUSION

The inevitable responsibility for the Black female scholar is to mold and shape her role within white institutions of higher learning. She has a unique position in that she must determine how she wants to be viewed because her small numbers have not set a precedent for her to follow. In white institutions, she will be faced with many stresses she had not anticipated. She will have to come to terms with recurring negative events. Her best coping strategy would be to work hard, keep a realistic perspective, and document her experiences so that others who follow her might learn.

REFERENCES

Banks, W.M. (1984). Afro-American scholars in the university: Roles and conflicts. *American Behavioral Scientist*, 27(3), 325–338.

Epstein, C.F. (1973). Positive effects of the multiple negative: Explaining the success of Black professional women. *American Journal of Sociology*, 78(4), 912–935.

Leggon, C. B. (1975). *The Black female professional: Role strains and status inconsistencies.* Unpublished doctoral dissertation, University of Chicago.

Moore, W., Jr., & Wagstaff, L.H. (1974). *Black educators in white colleges.* San Francisco: Jossey-Bass.

Painter, N. (1981, Dec. 10). Hers. *New York Times*, p. 22.

Pearlin, L.I. (1980). Life-strains and psychological distress among adults. In N.J. Smegler & E.H. Erikson (Eds.), *Themes of work and love in adulthood.* Cambridge, MA: Harvard University Press.

Schlossberg, N.K. (1984). *Counseling adults in transition: Linking practice with theory.* New York: Springer Publishing Co.

■ two
INDIVIDUAL ISSUES AND SOLUTIONS

■ 7
Challenges during the Transition from Graduate Student to Assistant Professor

JANICE D. YODER

Women with doctoral degrees consistently are underrepresented in the upper echelons of the academic hierarchy. As recently as 1979–1980, only 9.8% of Ph.D. full professors in colleges and universities, 19.4% of associate professors, 33.9% of assistant professors, and a full 51.8% of instructors were women (Andersen, 1981). In 1980–1981, 31% of the doctoral degrees awarded across all fields were earned by women, while fully one-half of all master's and bachelor's degrees were attained by women (Grant & Snyder, 1983).

In most fields, a consistent pattern exists showing a steady decline in the representation of women from the B.A. to the M.A. and Ph.D. For example, 44% of B.A.s awarded in the social sciences in 1980 went to women, 38% of the M.A.s and 27% of the doctoral degrees. The same pattern is evident in mathematics (43%, 34%, 16%), engineering (10%, 8%, 4%), business and management (37%, 25%, 15%) and psychology (65%, 58%, 43%). The overall equality of women and men at the master's level is the result of an overconcentration of women in traditionally "feminine" fields, such as the health professions (74% of all master's degrees awarded in this field in 1980 went to women), education (71%), and library science (83%).

Why do women cluster in the lower levels of academe, becoming more and more scarce as we progress up the professional hierarchy? There are two potential answers to this question: personal and structural (Riger & Galligan, 1980). *Personal* explanations focus on individual characteristics as reasons why women do not compete successfully with men. In this view, academe is regarded as a meritocracy, in which the career ladder is equally accessible to all qualified candidates. Women's lack of advancement can be explained by gender differences that make them less equipped to succeed. Recommendations for change, according to this approach, would focus on changing the individual to fit the situation; for example, advice to women academics would urge them to "act more like men," in order to advance, that is, to publish more or be more aggressive.

Research on how well personal factors explain women's position in academe is equivocal. Data on the promotion of women in psychology illustrates the controversy. Success in this field, as in most academic areas, is determined by quantity and quality of publications, time in administrative positions, type of employing institution, job mobility, and continuity of work experiences (Emmons, 1982). Evidence that women publish less frequently (Astin, 1972) and are cited less often than men (Emmons, 1982; Helmreich, Spence, Beane, Lucker, & Matthews, 1980) is contradicted by other studies indicating that women publish equal numbers of papers (Teghtsoonian, 1974) of comparable quality (Over, 1981). Women are less likely than men to be exposed to administrative experiences (Astin, 1972). Although more married women consider job mobility to be problematic for themselves than do married men (Reagan, 1975), Emmons (1982) finds that actual mobility is not related to promotion for either men or women. Finally, concerning continuity of work experience, Astin (1972) reported that 79% of women doctorates have never interrupted their careers.

Structural explanations, in contrast to personal ones, focus on environmental factors in academe which systematically discriminate against women as reasons for our lack of advancement. Inequities in the structure of the academic environment itself can be viewed as filters which eliminate women at each level of the academic hierarchy. The first filter system may be admissions to graduate education, which accept fewer women at each level of training.

Structural biases against women can be used to explain the same phenomena attributed to personal causes. For example, women indeed may be more likely than men to be employed part-time, but this may be the consequence of biases against hiring women during their reproductive years (a structural explanation), instead of women's inability to take a full-time position due to child-rearing demands (a personal explanation). Similarly, women may not fill administrative roles because the selection process is biased against them, not because they do not seek these appointments (personal explanation).

Personal explanations tend to blame victims. Women in the professions who want to succeed, according to these explanations, should abandon desires for familial bonds and learn to exhibit the masculine characteristics associated with administrators. However, there are a number of structural factors which could prevent such strategies from succeeding. In this chapter, I will discuss the structural barriers women experience — the second set of filters — as they make the transition from graduate student to assistant professor.

GRADUATE SCHOOL

All of us have been students at some point in our lives and we know the role well. As students, we were passive, deferential, and externally evaluated. Men and women play this role in equal numbers (Grant, 1983), which attests to the gender neutrality of this role. However, fewer women receive doctoral degrees. Why do women suddenly become underrepresented at the advanced level?

Changes in role demands may answer this question in part. The student role changes significantly when graduates are A.B.D. (all but dissertation). With classes behind them, doctoral candidates take on a new role, that of apprentice to a profession. Now, the game includes publishing, networking, and public speaking, which take confidence, assertiveness, and the support of mentors. This may be the first time in a woman's academic career when she is confronted with role conflicts. Two barriers I encountered in graduate school at this stage of my own career development were, first, a paucity of female mentors and, second, lack of support for my career development.

The existence of few women mentors is the result of a downward spiral: with few women in the upper academic ranks, there are few mentors to show women how to manage their sex role and professional role. To a novice for whom the new demands of a dissertation are inconsistent with her sex-role expectations and prior experiences, this inability to find mentors (or to choose among a limited array) can be discouraging.

In my case, I was in a department with equal numbers of male and female students but with only one of eight faculty in my area who was a woman. This lone woman was expected to help all the women students as well as weather her own tenure review. Needless to say, she was not a reliable source of support.

Even when women are granted tenure, it often is in token numbers; only 19.4% of Associate Professors are women (Andersen, 1981). Tokens are marginal, underrepresented members of a work group (Kanter, 1977; Laws, 1975). Because of their proportionally small numbers, tokens stand out from the other members of the work group. Their visibility can create performance pressures and their difference from others makes people uncertain about how to treat them. Often these uncertainties are resolved by encapsulating tokens into stereotypic sex roles such as "mother" or "seductress." If junior women play token roles, mentoring relationships are so inhibited that even established women are unlikely to offer sponsorship to less advanced women (Yoder, Adams, Grove, & Priest, 1985).

My second point is more difficult to document yet it seems to reflect the sentiments of many women doctoral candidates. I believe that faculty do not treat women's career aspirations with the same seriousness with which they respond to male colleagues. I was part of a group of five women students who clustered together and struggled to format our vitae, meet people at professional meetings, discuss jobs, and share dissertation ideas. At the same time, we watched our male peers banter with faculty members about their dissertation over a beer, travel to meetings with their advisers, and consider postdoctoral work to enhance their marketability. Although our women's support group was invaluable, we certainly did not possess the expertise embodied by the faculty and shared with our male counterparts.

All this occurred in a department with balanced numbers of women and men that can best be characterized as nonsupportive rather than negative or hostile. When a department is dominated by male students and faculty, male faculty express the most negative attitudes toward women (Holahan, 1979). In a sex-balanced department, negative attitudes do not vanish, but they are mitigated. In any case, these attitudes contribute a stress in graduate school that is shouldered inequitably by women.

BECOMING A PROFESSIONAL

After completing graduate school, the next career step is to acquire an academic job. Affirmative action laws are supposed to ensure equal opportunity in hiring. In fact some data seem to bear this out; for example, comparable percentages of women and men doctorates and masters employed full-time in psychology are distributed equally across community colleges, four-year institutions, and universities (Stapp & Fulcher, 1981). However, other problems may arise with affirmative action, networking, and sexual harassment.

One abuse of affirmative action regulations which is rumored to occur is that women may be interviewed superficially only to fulfill these requirements and/or hired to fill temporary positions to increase artificially the sex ratio of a department. Of course, the converse is frequently touted by opponents of affirmative action who feel that it gives women an unfair advantage. (This opinion ignores the fact that current employees benefited from the systematic exclusion of female and minority competitors from past job searches.) For a revealing look at one university's struggle with affirmative action, see Macaulay (1981).

The reported existence of an exclusive "old-boy" network is another area of concern for female job applicants. In a study of recruitment practices by employers registered at the annual meetings of the Eastern Psychological Association, 24% of the respondents admitted to having a candidate in mind for the job prior to coming to the meetings (Kessler, McKenna, Russell, Stang, & Sweet, 1976). Furthermore, 74% reported relying on friends and colleagues for recommendations of viable job candidates in at least some instances, and a full 30% of positions reportedly were filled in this way. If anything, social desirability influences might cause these figures to be underestimates. In any case, networks do exist and access to them enhances one's marketability.

Women appear to have less access to these networks. Denmark (1980) reports that status, not gender, is the most important factor in determining how many links a person needs to contact a target person. However, gender is influential in the linkages themselves. Those who have access to high-status men and women are likely to be men. In other words, if I wanted to contact a high-status person through someone both he or she and I knew, the intermediate contact probably would be a man.

Another area where women are most likely to be treated differently from their male counterparts is in cases of sexual harassment. This can occur at any stage of a woman's career when she is in a less powerful and dependent position (Somers, 1982), such as when she is a job applicant. In such cases, the harasser's expectations concerning the victim's sexuality and vulnerability color the professional relationship. The victim is no longer regarded by the perpetrator as a colleague, job candidate, or student, but rather as a stereotypic female (i.e., less powerful) sex object. This is one of the strongest possible affronts to a woman's professional role development.

Although there is no generally accepted definition of sexual harassment, harassing behaviors may include "verbal harassment, leering, offensive sexual remarks, unwanted touching, subtle pressure for sexual activity, overt demands for sexual activity, and physical assualt" (Somers, 1982, p. 28). All of these involve coercion on the part of the perpetrator (Reilly, Carpenter, Dull, & Bartlett, 1982). For working women, estimates of the incidence of harassment range from 20 to 60%, depending on the definition of harassment used (Brewer, 1982).

I was sexually harassed during my first job. I was told directly by a tenured faculty member that my tenuous one-year visiting position would continue more readily if I slept with him. My reactions ranged from initial self-blame to deep-seated anger and resentment. Like others, I felt emotionally and physically stressed, less satisfied with my job, and less willing to collaborate with my colleagues (Jensen & Gutek, 1982; Livingston, 1982).

Victims of sexual harassment most frequently elect to avoid or ignore the perpetrator, although ignoring the problem is not effective in eliminating it (Silverman, 1976). Other victims, like myself, talk to their supervisors, and they report that this action is most likely to "make things better" (Livingston, 1982). In addition to individual solutions, structural protections (grievances) and legal recourse also help to take responsibility away from the victim. However, they cannot adequately compensate women for the loss of self-esteem and identity as a professional. Nor is the right to a harassment-free work place guaranteed.

CONCLUSION

What some regard as the career ladder for academics may actually be a filter system which eliminates women at each step of the academic hierarchy. The filter system is structurally biased, imposing barriers for women based on gender roles, not ability. A recognition of the structural barriers women face has two major benefits. First, it pinpoints precisely what aspects of the environment will have to be changed in order to promote women's advancement, such as finding more mentors or protecting them from sexual harassment. Second, it encourages the individual woman to look for external factors to explain her position, instead of internalizing the blame for sex discrimination.

REFERENCES

Andersen, C.J. (1981). *1981–1982 Fact book for academic administrators.* Washington, DC: American Council on Education.

Astin, H. (1972). Employment and career status of women psychologists. *American Psychologist, 27,* 371–381.

Brewer, M.B. (1982). Further beyond nine to five: An integration and future directions. *Journal of Social Issues, 38,* 149–158.

Denmark, F.L. (1980). Psyche: From rocking the cradle to rocking the boat. *American Psychologist, 35,* 1057–1065.

Emmons, C.A. (1982). A longitudinal study of the careers of a cohort of assistant professors in psychology. *American Psychologist, 37,* 1228–1238.

Grant, W. V. (1983). *Digest of education statistics 1983–84.* Washington, DC: National Center for Education Statistics.

Helmreich, R.L., Spence, J.T., Beane, W.E., Lucker, G.W., & Matthews, K.A. (1980). Making it in academic psychology: Demographic and personality correlates of attainment. *Journal of Personality and Social Psychology, 39,* 896–908.

Holahan, C.K. (1979). Stress experienced by women doctoral students, need for support, and occupational sex typing: An interactional view. *Sex Roles, 5,* 425–436.

Jensen, I., & Gutek, B. (1982). Attributions and assignment of responsibility for sexual harassment. *Journal of Social Issues, 38,* 121–136.

Kessler, S., McKenna, W., Russell, V., Stang, D.J., & Sweet, S. (1976). The job market in psychology: A survey of despair. *Personality and Social Psychology Bulletin, 2,* 22–26.

Kanter, R.M. (1977). *Men and women of the corporation.* New York: Basic Books.

Laws, J.L. (1975). The psychology of tokenism: An analysis. *Sex Roles, 1,* 209–223.

Livingston, J.A. (1982). Responses to sexual harassment on the job. *Journal of Social Issues, 38,* 5–22.

Macaulay, J. (1981). The failure of affirmative action for women: One university's experience. In G. Desole & L. Hoffman (Eds.), *Rocking the boat* (pp. 98–116). New York: Modern Language Association of America.

Over, R. (1981). Representation of women on the editorial boards of psychology journals. *American Pychologist, 36,* 885–891.

Reagan, B.R. (1975). Two supply curves for economists? Implications of mobility and career attainment of women. *American Economic Review, 65,* 92–99.

Reilly, T., Carpenter, S., Dull, V., & Bartlett, K. (1982). The factorial survey technique: An approach to defining sexual harassment on campus. *Journal of Social Issues, 38,* 99–110.

Riger, S., & Galligan, P. (1980). Women in management: An exploration of competing paradigms. *American Psychologist, 35,* 902–910.

Silverman, D. (1976). Sexual harassment: Working women's dilemma. *Quest: A Feminist Quarterly, 3,* 15–24.

Somers, A. (1982). Sexual harassment in academe: Legal issues and definitions. *Journal of Social Issues, 38,* 23–32.

Stapp, J., & Fulcher, R. (1981). The employment of APA members. *American Psychologist, 36,* 1263–1314.

Teghtsoonian, M. (1974). Distribution by sex of authors and editors of psychological journals, 1970–1972. *American Psychologist, 29,* 262–269.

Yoder, J.D., Adams, J., Grove, S., & Priest, R.F. (1985). To teach is to learn: Reducing tokenism with mentors. *Psychology of Women Quarterly, 9,* 119–131.

■ 8
Lessons from My First Job

KATHRYN QUINA

When I review those five long years at my first academic post, I realize that they were not completely wasted. I learned a lot about academic standards and procedures, about harassment, and about support. The attacks on my values, my intellectual style, and my femaleness/feminism led me to a more enduring and sophisticated system of beliefs, as I was forced to justify my priorities and to stand up for my values. It also led me to look for a more satisfying job. But I did waste a lot of valuable time trying to figure out who was wrong, me or my colleagues, and what to do about either case. In hope of reducing similar wasted efforts by others, I offer the following lessons for emotional as well as professional survival and success.

LESSON 1: KEEP GOOD WRITTEN RECORDS

Keep a journal of your experiences on a regular basis. Describe all academic achievements and activities such as speaking or community service, and make your positive contributions public. Detail incidents that make you uncomfortable in the work place, including comments made about your work or yourself; include names and dates. Whenever possible, further document unprofessional behavior involving others in the form of a specific and dated memo or letter, and send it to the offender or to your chair or dean. Keep minutes or your own notes from meetings, and any memos that concern you or your position. Ask for verbal comments (good or bad) to be confirmed in writing.

LESSON 2: EVALUATE YOURSELF HONESTLY, WITHOUT PREJUDICE

Because your male peers are likely to be overvalued, it may be difficult to assess your own status. Your own prejudice probably is that you are never meeting those stringent internal standards you've set. (Relax — you probably won't, but neither will anybody else.) The peer review process adds another prejudice: your weaknesses are always pointed out, but your strengths often pass without comment.

Measure yourself against the written records of your peers, usually available during reviews. Bear in mind that different people have different strengths, and consider your overall record. Don't allow yourself to be hurt by "pot shots"; hostility against you probably means you're doing well enough to be taken seriously. The best you can do is to respond to reasonable suggestions for improvement with sincere effort, and to react to unfair criticisms with your more realistic assessment.

LESSON 3: FIND A GOOD FEMINIST SUPPORT GROUP

I was told, as you may be, to stay away from "those feminists," because it would "look bad" on your record. Don't listen. Join your local academic and professional women's group, go to Women's Studies meetings even if you do not specialize in Women's Studies, and connect with other women on campus. Attend meetings and work with regional and national groups. (See chapter by Rose on networks for further suggestions.) There you can find role-models of success, of struggle, and of survival. I also found support and sympathy, insight and information. I learned that my experiences were not unique and developed a new perspective on the causes of my problems with colleagues. Finally, I developed the skills for solving, or at least working on, some of the bothersome patterns of discrimination I was facing and, most importantly, the courage to proceed with those solutions. The people I met and the data I gathered in those feminist networks continue to be my most valuable resources, personally and professionally.

And those warnings about my future? I discovered why they didn't want me to join "those groups:" they had given me a new power base.

No one ever mentioned my feminist activities again, except in commendations on my "exceptional service record." The experience, skills, and insight I gained from my feminist support group activities became the keys to my future.

LESSON 4: KNOW YOUR RIGHTS

Discrimination is still rampant, so it is especially important that you look out for yourself with legal protection. Read your contract and the grievance procedures within your institution. If you have a union or academic group like the American Association of University Professors, find out more about their role (joining their grievance committee is an excellent way). You can find out about national actions through sources like the *Chronicle of Higher Education.*

Involve a union/organization representative in evaluation procedures as soon as you suspect that grievable action is taking place. Don't hesitate to file a grievance after an unfavorable decision, and to seek your union/organization's support. They are there for your protection, whether they agree personally with your case or not, so utilize their resources.

LESSON 5: SPEAK UP!

Another collegial voice of doom warned me, "Stay quiet and tow the line. If you're a troublemaker, they will get rid of you." For two years I was silent, while things got worse. Finally an unfair evaluation forced me to assert my legal rights. To my amazement, the very fact that I called my colleagues on their action, publicly and knowledgeably, created a dramatic turnaround in their treatment of me. Once they knew that I knew what was happening, they apparently figured they couldn't get away with so much. My next three years were louder and yet more peaceful. Of course, speaking up involves risks, but suffering in silence does not seem to be the best way to stop mistreatment.

LESSON 6: DEFINE CLEAR BOUNDARIES ABOUT SEXUAL BEHAVIOR

A simple statement about unacceptable behavior, such as "I don't have sex with my colleagues," or "I am committed to another relationship" seems to work the best. Bounding social relationships by a rule that applies to everyone will stop some propositions and avoid hurt feelings among those who try anyway. If a sexual approach continues, you should pursue a complaint of sexual harassment.

If you choose to have a sexual relationship with a colleague, make sure it is on an equal basis and worth the risk; even a voluntary affair can be used as evidence against your stability or character.

LESSON 7: CULTIVATE STUDENT RESPECT AND SUPPORT

Students' voices rarely overrule faculty personnel decisions, but positive student input can have an impact on those decisions. Student support is best achieved by being fair, honest, and caring. It may take years to develop a good reputation, but the energy you devote to teaching and working with students will be well repaid.

LESSON 8: DON'T FALL INTO THE PSYCHOLOGY OF THE "TOKEN"

If you are alone in a category, you will be subjected to special burdens: "you only got your job because you're xx;" "you have an edge because you can cry discrimination;" "if you fail/leave/stay, we'll never hire another xx." Ignore them. You wouldn't be there if you weren't qualified. But if someone believes those stereotypes, not much you can do will change their mind anyway. Instead, make your goal to do the best you can — after all, that's all they're asking of the nontokens! Meanwhile, write all those comments down in your journal, because collecting them will help you recognize and document tokenism, which is discrimination.

LESSON 9: EVALUATE YOUR OWN PRIORITIES

Do not forget that your evaluations will hinge primarily on your publication record. You should refuse to get sidetracked with laborious tasks that will not lead to tangible lines in the right places on your vita. If your department asks you to do an onerous course or unrewarded task, check out the offer. If everyone else has refused it, you have the same right. Use your need to work on your research as your reason for declining the honor (though you might promise your services after you're promoted!).

On the other hand, you don't need to give up nonresearch opportunities that have other benefits. Time devoted to improvement of your teaching, or for service activities that lead to new skills or professional contacts, is usually rewarded in less direct but no less important ways.

LESSON 10: IF IT IS NOT RIGHT FOR YOU, MOVE ON

If you are unhappy, you owe it to yourself to examine your options. When you feel "stuck" in your job, you are the most vulnerable to abuse. Send your vita out, register for job placement services, and attend workshops and seminars on alternative careers. In my third year, I realized that staying would be worse for my mental health than leaving, even if I had to change some of my dreams about my future. By starting early, I had the luxury of looking while working. It was two years before I accepted a new position. I did lose a couple of years toward tenure and some salary, but I found a place where my work was appreciated, and it was well worth the wait. Others have found greater satisfaction by moving off the tenure track into industry, administration, or consulting.

I've talked to a number of people who have left unhappy situations, some involuntarily, who invariably found the change beneficial and wondered why they took so long to move. I have also observed the tragedy of lives for those who don't have the courage to leave or the luck to be fired. This last group succeeded in the departmental battlefields, but at the expense of themselves as persons.

CONCLUSIONS

Along the way to these lessons, I experienced self-doubt, physical and emotional stress, and little failures. But I have also felt the joy of my successes, from small system improvements to great personal victories. Most important, I have emerged with self-respect. Hopefully, these lessons can help make your professional goals easier to attain, and your personal goals and happiness harder to lose.

■ 9
The Graduate School Experience

LINDA ROGERS

Graduate school can be the best of times, and the worst of times (with apologies to Charles Dickens). On the positive side, there is the opportunity to study in the field you love and have chosen as your life's work. You also will have the freedom to function more or less independently, an abundance of cultural and intellectual stimulation, and a chance to meet and interact with professionals in your field. On the negative side, graduate school involves a heavy work load, often accompanied by high levels of emotional and financial stress.

THE INITIAL ADJUSTMENT

The initial adjustment to graduate school can be very difficult as students experience multiple life changes. It is not unusual, for example, to move to a new town, if not an entirely different part of the country, leaving behind familiar places, old friends, family, and support networks. For those entering graduate school directly from an undergraduate institution, the change involves new, undefined roles, a decrease in structure, and an increase in the quality of work expected. For many younger graduate students, this also may be a period of intense personal growth as they separate both physically and emotionally from their family. For older students, the return to school may involve a drastic change in financial status, as well as the loss of prestige inherent in the move from full-time employee to full-time student. Older graduate students may worry that they will not be able to compete with their younger colleagues, and some may have the additional responsibility of child care.

For all students there is the stress of testing one's competence, of competing with other excellent students, and of being continually evaluated by the faculty. Most graduate students have been the "stars" of their undergraduate classes, and the adjustment to being only one of many "stars" can be disappointing and difficult. All of these major transitions occur at once, in the first weeks of graduate training. It's no wonder that first semester students report feeling "shell-shocked," overwhelmed by the necessary emotional adjustments.

While the major adjustments occur during the first year, other sources of stress are present throughout graduate training. Research, advanced seminars, teaching, public speaking, comprehensive exams, practicums, and internships can be frightening and overwhelming. Although mastery of these tasks will increase confidence gradually, anxieties related to being constantly evaluated really do not ever disappear.

THE SHIFT FROM COURSEWORK TO DISSERTATION

The shift from coursework to dissertation research is often traumatic for several reasons. The dissertation is usually the last hurdle before one achieves the degree and takes on the unknown role of professional person. With only one more major project to complete, one's fears of failure, fears of success, and feelings of being an impostor rise to the fore. This may be especially true for women, who might have difficulty believing in their own competence or who are struggling to make their professional identity a priority in their life. It's easy at this point to find lots of very good reasons to do something — anything — other than the dissertation, particularly if a woman has unresolved conflicts about making career goals foremost.

These internal anxieties can be compounded by a decrease in external support from the department. Students who are A.B.D. (all but dissertation) are frequently not supported financially and, because they may be physically absent due to internships or jobs, sometimes find themselves without the emotional support of old friends. A.B.D.s often describe feelings of loss and estrangement when they return to the department to find only a few old friends and lots of new faces.

At a time when students particularly need faculty support and guidance, professors may subtly change their attitudes toward them. By the dissertation stage of graduate school, faculty will be expecting students to behave more as a colleague than as students. It is best to be prepared to work as independently as possible.

Attitudes about supervising dissertations will vary among faculty. Faculty members have their own memories of surviving the dissertation, and may react accordingly. Some may think that students should have it as tough as they did (e.g., final approval of the dissertation should take years and the process should be painful). Others may see the dissertation research as a character-building process in which some suffering is necessary. Most are simply busy with their own lives. A rare few will enjoy directing a dissertation.

Probably the most significant cause of stress for many A.B.D.s is the fact that a dissertation is an entirely new type of task, and it looks absolutely overwhelming. Nothing in the past years of schooling has really prepared a graduate student for this type of major, long-term, creative effort. Academic work from grade school through graduate coursework typically does not demand critical, original thinking. With the possible exceptions of the Master's thesis or extensive research experience, nothing has prepared most students for the quality of thinking required by a dissertation.

Not only is the nature of the task vastly different from most course requirements, but the very scope of writing a dissertation and the time commitment involved is unlike anything previously encountered. It's like switching from running sprints to running cross-country. The basic activity may be the same, but all the strategies and techniques are different. In addition, for women who are unresolved about professional versus family roles, the need to make the dissertation a top priority will be a source of conflict that may impede progress. For a thorough discussion and lots of helpful hints on surviving the dissertation, *How to Complete and Survive a Doctoral Dissertation* (Sternberg, 1981) is strongly recommended.

COPING SKILLS

Building Support Networks

Despite the difficulties involved, many women do survive graduate school and have discovered some techniques that increase one's ability to cope. The most important coping skill is that of building relationships. Graduate students who report supportive relationships with faculty and peers have been found to have significantly less physical and emotional distress during the first year of graduate school than students who report less satisfying relationships (Goplerud, 1980).

A strong support network should consist of beneficial relationships with peers, with more advanced students, with friends outside the graduate program who support your intellectual endeavors, and with the faculty. You and your immediate peers may feel initially cautious and somewhat competitive toward one another. If you can overcome these initial feelings of insecurity long enough to provide mutual support and companionship, however, you'll find that the benefits are tremendous. The members of your "class" (the group of people who enter together) will struggle through all stages of the program at the same time and can become a great source of intellectual stimulation and comfort for one another.

No one else will be able to understand so exactly or commiserate so completely as those who are in the same circumstance at the same time. Some programs have instituted a weekly discussion for first-year students to serve as a more structured support system. In these groups it is important that the leader be someone who has no evaluative power over the students and who can act as mentor and facilitator. Misery does love company, and besides, you won't feel so bad about that exam or paper if others are worried too. So take the first step, risk some self-disclosure, and try to develop a spirit of unity among your classmates. You're all in this together!

Relationships with more advanced students can be beneficial to you in a slightly different way. Although these students can also commiserate and provide emotional support, more importantly they can act as models or mentors, providing you with inside information and advice not available elsewhere. For example, advanced students can clue you in to the history and politics of the department, enabling you to avoid becoming involved in power struggles that have little or nothing to do with you. They can advise you of temperamental differences in faculty and show you the ropes when it comes to making crucial decisions such as choosing an advisor or a dissertation committee. They can warn you whether a particular faculty member is prone to sexual harassment. They also are potential research collaborators and academic resources. As Rose points out in an earlier chapter, your graduate network is an important part of the national network you will need to develop if you wish to work for tenure in academe or seek jobs outside it.

Finally, relationships with members of the faculty can provide you not only with information and skills, but also with a special type of support, encouragement, models of professional behavior, information and advice about your future in the field, and professional contacts. You are not, of course, going to "hit it off" with every professor. It's important to cultivate good, supportive working relationships with one or two whom you admire, and who seem to like you, at the same time establishing a reputation for yourself with all faculty members as a hardworking, responsible individual.

A potential hazard in this area involves the problem of the appropriate distance between faculty and students. The difficulty lies in the fact that professors have differing ideas of what is "appropriate." Some prefer a good deal of distance in the teacher-student relationship, while others seem to forget or ignore differences in your respective positions, enjoying a closer, more personal interaction. This can be confusing. The best approach is probably one that includes, first, taking your cues for appropriate distance from the faculty member and, second, realizing that there *is* a difference in power in this relationship.

One final word of caution about faculty-student relationships. Working together closely, sharing personal experiences, and being mutually supportive often leads to sexual attraction between teacher and student. However, in many cases, the adverse consequences for the student of a professor-graduate student romance " . . . far outweigh the potential for emotional or professional growth" (Schover, Levenson, & Pope, 1983, p. 282). Although a sexual relationship can ultimately be harmful to both individuals, it is far more likely to be the student who suffers. As a student, you depend on the goodwill of the faculty for general student evaluations, course grades, research advice and approval, and letters of recommendation. Involving yourself in a romantic relationship with a faculty member jeopardizes all of these, as well as the respect you receive from other professors.

Find Your Personal Working Style

An important function of graduate school is to mold serious, committed academic professionals out of sometimes less serious, less committed students. In the process of this transformation, students often find it necessary to reorganize and rethink their style of working. For example, the last-minute flurry to slap together a paper the day before the due date might have worked all right during undergraduate days. In graduate courses that method may not be so effective. Certainly it will never get you through the dissertation. Thus it becomes important to discover a working style that is efficient, productive, and — yes — even enjoyable.

There are many popular books available on time management and self-management that will help you if you have difficulty setting priorities. Two aimed specifically at women are *Super Self: A Woman's Guide to Self-Management* (Tennov, 1977) and *Time In, Time Out, Time Enough: A Time Management Guide for Women* (Materka, 1977). Also recommended is *Working It Out* (Ruddick & Daniels, 1977), which includes fascinating essays by 23 women professionals.

When revising and reorganizing work habits, the important factors to keep in mind are the personal ones. Plan your work style around your own temperament, lifestyle, and needs. For example, are you a night person or a morning person? Plan to work on more difficult tasks when you are at your peak. Do you need large blocks of time — say two or three hours — or do you work better in short spurts of 15 to 20 minutes? Do you prefer some background noise or complete silence? Do you think best when surrounded by children and clutter, or do you require well-organized files and a tidy desk? Most writers recommend that you set aside a place reserved only for work, but one professional I know claims she works best sitting on the floor of the bathroom with the door locked. Force yourself to become aware of what working conditions are best for you, then deliberately structure your environment to maximize your effectiveness when working.

Lists and time schedules are suggested frequently to help maintain priorities. I find that I need a deadline to stay motivated, even if it's my own deadline and I know I can change it. It helps to know I want to do a specific section by a certain date. Some authors have recommended setting up a timetable for completion of the dissertation as soon as a topic is chosen. For some women, lists and time schedules provide needed structure. For others, deadlines increase anxiety to the point of paralysis, and a timetable that isn't followed exactly may only produce feelings of despair. Discover what works for you.

You also need to consider other obligations and relationships when you rethink your work style. You may want to disengage temporarily from some activities in order to focus on your work. This may be especially true while writing the dissertation. You may want to retain other activities and relationships, either for your sanity or because you feel responsible.

Political activity or feminist organizations may be a priority for you, for example, because you feel an obligation to participate or because they provide support. Similarly, partners, children, and other long-term relationships do not do well when ignored for long periods of time. Consider your outside obligations and relationships, and determine methods of tending to them without interfering with your commitment to your work.

Finding your own work style may be difficult, but it's worth the time and energy it takes. The struggle to develop work habits that are effective for you is in itself a statement that you see your work as important and deserving of some time, care, and attention.

Be Goal-directed

Whatever work style you evolve in graduate school, it will help to be as internally motivated as possible. In the process of taking required courses and conducting research, it is easy to lose sight of the fact that you are not in a program simply to please the faculty. You are there to learn, and thereby to advance your own career. You need not be passive in the process! Seek out experiences — courses, assistantships, internships, supervision, and types of research — that will lead you in the directions you have chosen for yourself. Make use of the faculty, the courses, and the experiences available to obtain the education *you* want. Graduate school will provide you with an unparalleled opportunity to immerse yourself in study and to develop beneficial colleague relationships. Be sure to take advantage of it.

Enjoy Yourself

Stress reduction, improved scholastic functioning, and your general mood can all be improved by taking (no — *making*) time to enjoy life. Continue your social, personal, and recreational pursuits as much as possible. Play raquetball, tennis, golf, or pinochle. Go to a play, a museum, or a rock concert. The point is to do something fun, something unrelated to graduate school.

It's OK to Feel Stressed

Graduate students are frequently under the impression that they should be paragons of mental health, especially if they are in psychology or social work. In competitive environments like graduate school, handling things well at all times thus becomes not only a goal, but also a criterion of one's value as a person, not to mention as a professional. One important tactic for increasing coping ability and decreasing distress is to give yourself permission to feel worried, upset, anxious. It's OK. Really! Accept your own human tendency to feel tense and to handle things in a less than perfect manner. If the stress becomes too great, don't be embarrassed to seek professional help.

SUMMARY

Although graduate school can be emotionally as well as physically exhausting, it can also be exciting and challenging. The discomfort and stress inherent in the process of graduate training can be mitigated by a strong support network among peers, advanced students, faculty, and others; an effective work style; a positive attitude based on an inner-directed pursuit of professional goals; active pursuit of enjoyable, non-academic activities; and an acceptance of one's own anxieties.

REFERENCES

Goplerud, E. N. (1980). Social support and stress during the first year of graduate school. *Professional Psychology, 11*(2), 283–290.

Materka, P. R. (1977). *Time in, time out, time enough: A time management guide for women.* Englewood Cliffs, NJ: Prentice-Hall.

Ruddick, S. & Daniels, P. (Eds.) (1977). *Working it out.* New York: Pantheon Books.

Schover, L. R., Levenson, H., & Pope, K. S. (1983). Sexual relationships in psychology training: A brief comment on ethical guidelines and coping strategies. *Psychology of Women Quarterly, 7*(3), 282–285.

Sternberg, D. (1981). *How to complete and survive a doctoral dissertation.* New York: St. Martin's Press.

Tennov, D. (1977). *Super self: A woman's guide to self-management.* New York: Jove.

■ 10
Middle-aged Women and Career Transitions

ROSALIE J. ACKERMAN

What is it like to change jobs in middle adulthood? How do middle-aged women handle such job transitions? What strategies do they use to change careers after obtaining a degree in their chosen or preferred fields? How will they endure the stress emanating from the dual roles of supermom and career woman?

Midlife career changes may involve reentry into academia or other structured vocational training. The returning woman student is becoming a familiar characteristic of the graduate school landscape. In my Midwestern training program, 62% of the incoming psychology graduate students were women over 30 who had experiences in the fields of history, English, teaching, and biochemistry. At my current university, 43% of the graduate students are women over 30. Acquaintances in my national professional network also indicate that the older student accounts for about 40% of admissions. Even if a woman already has obtained a graduate degree, there is still a high likelihood that she will change jobs in middle adulthood. Bolles (1984) estimates that most people change jobs a minimum of eight times in their lifetime.

How do middle-aged women handle these job transitions? One issue for reentry women is their indecision in changing major fields of study. Often, older women students experience anxiety, lower self-esteem, and a sense that they must make a career choice that agrees with significant others (Slaney & Dickson, 1985). They may need to be encouraged to consider different types of careers and perhaps to venture into new areas of interest (Badenhoop & Johansen, 1980; Brooks, 1976). On the other hand, the older-than-average student is more likely to have maturity and broad-ranging experiences, characteristics especially desirable in a graduate student.

My own career perspective has come from being a foods and nutrition specialist, a biochemist, a psychologist, and a neuropsychologist over a 20-year span. Further insight into job transition strategies comes from my research on a group of middle-aged women who were forced to change careers when a Midwestern company reorganized and eliminated 11% of the positions (Ackerman, in press). Certainly, the option of exercising choice in career change or in job seeking is preferable to being forced to make a transition. Even so, the issues surfacing in career changes for these women parallel ones for women over 30 who decide to earn the Ph.D. or to do postdoctoral retraining. The recommendations for making job transitions proposed later are based on my findings concerning which styles were most adaptive.

A STUDY OF COPING STYLES
DURING CAREER TRANSITIONS

The 71 women in my sample, ranging in age from 31 to 62, did not know whether their positions would be eliminated when the company they had been working for was reorganized in 1978. The typical participant was about 43 years old, married, with two children, and earning about $17,400 per year.

My interest was in determining what career strategies these women would use, given the possibility of losing their jobs. I postulated that the women would differ on two dimensions of job-changing behavior: (1) wanting to leave the job versus not wanting to leave it, and (2) planning versus not planning for the next job. I was able to classify the women into one of four categories based on different combinations of these two dimensions: want–plan, want–not plan, not want–plan, not want–not plan. Then, I determined how the coping styles of the four groups differed by examining their job-changing strategies, personality profiles, coping behaviors, stress levels, and job and life satisfaction. After assessing the groups, interpretive labels (creators, maintainers, conventionalists, and reacters, respectively) were assigned to each.

Not surprisingly, the most adaptive coping style was demonstrated by the women who both wanted and planned for a new job, the creators. Strategies and resources enabling the creators to weather the job-change transition were fourfold. First, most creators had financial resources, including access to annual incomes over $30,000. Second, they had supportive marriages: spouses aided with child rearing and household management and provided intimacy. However, some difficulties did exist with financial problems and in the marital relationships. Physical illness occurring among family members was a prominent problem in the family systems.

Third, creators had well-functioning outside support systems. Most had friends who were reassuring and willing to provide guidance and support that was vital in helping the women make positive adjustments during the transition. Community supports were essential for balancing the home, family, and work spheres. For instance, having backup lists of helpers for child-sitting helped to reduce anxiety. Professional networks were important at work to provide information, feedback about ideas, training in new jobs, and emotional support as the job change was managed.

Fourth, creators also had personality traits that benefited them. They were efficient in making decisions and felt good about what they had done. The women tended to be more inner-directed, and were highly motivated to pursue a career based on their own interests and desires. Creators also resorted to more self-help strategies to prepare for the job change: they enrolled in educational or retraining programs, sought career counseling, got individual or group therapy, or took assertiveness training courses. They also negotiated agreements with family members about household responsibilities. Nonetheless, creators experienced high levels of stress in their lives, and perhaps as a result tended to have frequent personal illnesses.

In contrast, the least adjusted group of women were the reacters. These women faced career transition without any desire or plans to change jobs. Family needs were a high priority for them, and they often expressed the perception that "others ran their lives." This external-directedness greatly decreased their sense of autonomy and of being respected by others, as well as their enjoyment of life. Their lives were chaotic. Of the four groups, they most frequently reported incidents of hostile behavior and physical complaints and illnesses by family members. Reacters reported extremely high stress levels.

Reacters were not very adaptive in terms of finding new ways to manage the transition facing them. Typically, they sought to change their work environment in concrete, simplistic ways. One woman, for example, sought to get a new office with a window; another tried to arrange a more favorable work shift. In general, reacters could not find anything positive about the career change.

Intermediate levels of psychological adjustment were evidenced by the maintainers, who wanted but hadn't planned for a new job, and conventionalists, who didn't want a new job but were planning for one. However, the two groups differed in several ways. Maintainers minimized the effects of the transition by asserting that "everything is okay" or "things are the same as they used to be." This denial or reframing of a stressful situation was carried to an extreme, and poorer psychological adjustment resulted. The women did not learn new ways to manage the problem facing them. Though their excessive optimism eased the stress, they reported being very anxious and had a high frequency of conflict with family members.

Rigidly held values about motherhood were characteristic of this style. In fact, maintainers tended to get pregnant more often than the others — perhaps to "resolve" the conflict about family and work roles. These women saw themselves as being other-directed most of the time, and generally felt they were not respected by others.

The conventionalists were more inner-directed and more flexible in their strategies than the maintainers. The women tried out new ways of managing the job transition, but only if they knew someone who had already tried it. Conventionalists' self-reported stress levels were as high as the creators'.

Family priorities were held in high regard by the conventionalists. Not surprisingly, they reported conflict between their career and family roles and experienced problems with their families, marriage, financial situation, and personal health, and frequently had legal difficulties. Their orthodox attitudes concerning woman's place in the family led to lowered self-esteem and a sense of not being highly regarded by others. Conventionalists did not enjoy life during the transition.

RECOMMENDATIONS FOR COPING STRATEGIES

One might speculate that most women graduate students or career changers would be creators, that is, would both want and plan a new career path. Unfortunately, this is not always the case. Because family problems, loss of a job, or other life events are sometimes the catalyst for change, a woman in midlife might find herself approaching the change as a maintainer, conventionalist, or reacter. For example, my transition from nutritionist to biochemist was in the style of the creators, but I would have been in the conventionalist group for the one from biochemist to psychologist. In the former, I wanted to increase my expertise in biochemistry as an extension of my interest in food and nutrition, and deliberately planned to get that training. However, the second career change occurred under different circumstances. I was in a dead-end job as a biochemist and had heavy family responsibilities which eventually forced me to leave my job. My ability to plan a career change was affected by the geographic limitations having a family imposed on me. My personal experience and my research both indicate that external factors often play a potent role for women who are changing jobs.

Clearly, exercising choice in leaving and procuring a job is preferable to being forced to make a career transition. Psychological adjustment is superior when choice is inherent in the transition, although stress levels are likely to be high, regardless. However, adjustment is greatly affected by each woman's coping style.

If you are considering a career change, you might want to reflect on your own coping style. Are you a creator or maintainer or conventionalist or reactor? A creative coping style has been associated with the best adjustment. Creative coping includes personal, psychological, and social resources which can be utilized to ease the strain of transitions. Indeed, career opportunities are significantly increased by creative coping strategies.

If you aren't already a creator, you might try to develop or acquire the resources associated with this style. First, the financial and emotional support of a spouse appears to be crucial. Social networks of friends, community members, and colleagues also provide emotional support as well as concrete help. Next, a moderate degree of optimism and a healthy sense of self-esteem ease the adjustment. Too little or too much optimism appears to be counterproductive, however. Finally, the keystone of the creative coping style is the ability to generalize old learning to new situations in ingenious, flexible ways. Creators seek out ways to train for new positions and use all resources at hand.

Consider these suggestions as you advance your career. How will you approach your next career transition — as a creator, maintainer, conventionalist, or reacter?

REFERENCES

Ackerman, R. J. (In press). Stress and concomitant coping strategies of middle-aged women changing jobs. *Women and Psychotherapy.*

Badenhoop, M., & Johansen, M. (1980). Do reentry women have special needs? *Psychology of Women Quarterly, 4,* 591–595.

Bolles, J. T. (1984). *What color is your parachute?* Berkeley, CA: Ten Speed Press.

Brooks, L. (1976). Supermoms shift gears: Re-entry women. *The Counseling Psychologist, 6,* 33–37.

Slaney, R., & Dickson, R. (1985). Relation of career indecision to career choice with reentry women: A treatment and follow-up study. *Journal of Counseling Psychology, 32,* 355–362.

■ 11
Black Women Clinicians:
Survival against the Odds

MARTHA E. BANKS

Black women frequently find themselves facing barriers in their job settings. In an economy characterized by high unemployment, discriminatory behavior is overt, with no fears of reprisal. Efforts to demoralize Black women are rampant; yet much of the discriminatory experience is invalidated by skepticism or outright denial. Even within the mental health fields, characterized publicly as "liberal," there is considerable disillusionment as we find ourselves facing discrimination in what one might expect to be a "safe" environment.

I have held professional staff positions in a variety of mental health settings, including community mental health centers, a nursing home, a private inpatient mental health center, and a federal medical hospital. Most of these positions have been in cities where the percentage of Black people is less than 4%, and the percentage of Black professionals significantly lower than that. In this chapter, I will describe some of the discrimination I have experienced as a Black woman clinician, and the techniques I have found helpful in managing under such difficult circumstances.

CREDIBILITY

One of the most serious problems you will confront as a Black woman Ph.D. is your lack of credibility as professional. You will frequently be in the position of being the "first" and/or the "only" Black woman at your job level. Under these conditions, other people on the staff might be skeptical about your status. For instance, I try to keep myself prepared for the unpredictable times when a new staff person (usually a clerk or secretary) asks me publicly, "Doctor, exactly what *are* your qualifications?" or "Are you a *real* doctor?" Other professionals also might ask you to justify your credentials.

Working in a setting with a hierarchical, racially segregated work force is also likely to affect Black women's professional credibility. In my present work setting, a majority of the lower-ranking jobs are held by Black employees, including nursing aides, housekeeping staff, and dietary staff. These employees are required to wear uniforms; there are relatively few Blacks who are in street clothes on the job. On occasion, I've been asked why I don't wear a uniform. To be stereotyped at a glance as "not a professional" based on race puts Black women, compared to white professionals, at a definite disadvantage.

To establish your credibility as a professional in this situation, it might be necessary to remind others of your credentials. This can be accomplished by using your title as much as possible. Remember, you earned it! In many clinical teaching facilities, such as hospitals, titles are considered very important. Or if identification badges use names but not titles, you could purchase a name plate for yourself, with your title on it. You might also want a professional name plate for your desk, with your title, name, and your position and/or highest credential. Another strategy is to introduce yourself to patients and staff by your title. Similarly, address others by title until *truly* casual relationships develop. However, pay attention to the level of casualness within the setting, in order to avoid being the only person using a title when others, with the same credentials, are using first names.

Keeping a high professional profile also will help legitimize your authority. Be ready to discuss professional issues or activities with colleagues. Attend professional meetings and keep abreast of current developments. Present lectures or workshops at other facilities — gratuitously, if necessary. When people in your work setting learn of such activity, it will enhance your professional status.

Conversely, avoid accepting any responsibilities that are not in keeping with your status. Though it may be hard to believe, professional Black women are *still* being asked to perform secretarial or domestic chores on the job. For example, instead of calling in the staff secretary, I have been asked to take notes during meetings and to keep the coffee pot clean, even though I am not a coffee drinker.

VISIBILITY

Another major issue with which Black women must contend is the unwelcome visibility associated with being a minority. Try to get used to the fact that you *will* be noticed. Personal characteristics, whether related to your job performance or not, will be subject to more intense scrutiny than majority group white women or men. Living in a "fishbowl" means that even your casual interactions, demeanor, and appearance will be observed and judged. For example, after seeing me talking to Black co-workers, white co-workers have made comments like "I saw you talking to so-and-so the other day," and "What were you conspiring about?" These comments not only reveal how uncomfortable whites may feel around Blacks, but also undermines the ease with which Blacks can form relationships. One way to diffuse such comments is to welcome the white co-worker to join the conversation.

I also have been asked whether or not I was providing psychotherapy to Black co-workers with whom I had conversations, but this question has never been raised about my interactions with white people. On several occasions, this query has been accompanied by a derogatory remark about the person to whom I was speaking, combined with a flattering statement like "He (or she) really needs help, and you're just the right person to provide it." The message is that it's okay for me to talk with Black co-workers as long as the conversation is under the guise of therapy, thereby eliminating any possiblity of social, personal, or professional aspects of normal conversation. I have countered such remarks with statements such as "I'm speaking to you right now, and I don't believe this is a therapy session we're having."

As a Black woman, your presence or absence, style of dress, and even mood will draw attention. Making yourself available in informal settings can be to your advantage. People will notice if you don't wish to socialize with them. Eating frequently at the work cafeteria or in a neighborhood restaurant that is popular with other employees affords them the chance to become familiar with you. Addressing other people by name on casual meeting indicates your interest in them. Professionalism and increased opportunities for personal interaction can be achieved by arriving slightly early for meetings and chatting with others before business gets underway.

If you are the first or only Black woman on the staff, other workers might not feel comfortable with you. Even if this discomfort is mutual, it will be to your advantage to overcome it by being as friendly and open to developing relationships as you can. As a member of a treatment team, for example, it is necessary for you to be able to work with other members for the benefit of the patient. It is important to build a support network within the work setting. Some ways to get involved include joining a common interest or study group, attending inservices (even if the topics are not of specific interest to you), or joining the credit union, optional professional staff meetings, or ad hoc committees to plan informal gatherings.

DISCRIMINATION

Discrimination against Black women is a major obstacle to professional survival. Others you work with may regard you as a threat. If your supervisor feels this way, you may experience difficulty in receiving credit for your work or perhaps even find your job in jeopardy. This happened to me one time when I was responsible for preparing preliminary results for an in-house research project. At the first meeting, my supervisor repeatedly turned to me for the answers to questions other staff members asked. Later, he informed me that the follow-up meeting had been postponed. However, I soon learned that the meeting time had *not* been changed, but that my supervisor went and presented my work to the executive committee as if it were his. Although it is difficult to sense similar situations before they occur, to assure that you get the credit you deserve, you should maintain copies of your work and create opportunities to discuss it with others.

To prevent other forms of discrimination, it is wise to protect yourself legally as much as possible. Try to get a written contract before accepting a position, if you can. If there are no contracts (or if *you* don't have one), keep a copy of your job description as published in the policy manual. Keep everything in writing. Read the policy manuals that pertain to your position. In one of my previous work settings, I discovered that the job description in the policy manual had very little resemblance to the position as it had been advertised. My attempts to perform what I believed were my duties as a professional were actually tantamount to insubordination. Such discrepancies between actual job duties and those presented prior to hiring serve to provide nonsupportive supervisors with opportunities for undue disciplinary action. This "noncompliance" is then given as an excuse to avoid future hiring of minorities and/or women. Unfortunately for the Black woman, this puts the burden on her not only to manage her own work load, but to serve as a constant representative for other minorities and women.

If your duties are severely restricted, find ways to expand your professional interactions. Having assumed additional responsibilities may protect you if your job is eliminated. If you're a clinician, try to teach, volunteer to provide inservice training, or supervise students (in any field).

Some ways to protect yourself legally are to:

1. Find out about Equal Employment Opportunity and Affirmative Action offices within the agency. Volunteer for committee work.
2. Keep a written record of problems, and maintain a copy away from the work site.
3. Ask questions of both personnel officers and supervisors.
4. Ascertain the agency policy on lines of communication through supervisors and co-workers.
5. Consider joining a union if that provides protection. Find loopholes that could endanger your position.
6. Pay particular attention to information on the grievance process. Check with co-workers about the efficacy of grievances. Be prepared to avoid grievances if you are in a position with few options, for example, when alternate employment is not available and there is limited mobility within the agency.

The federal government also provides guidelines for processing complaints of discrimination, including assigning to complainants an Equal Employment Opportunity Counselor who is responsible for gathering information from all parties in an attempt to resolve the issue. There are clearly defined time limits within which the processing of discrimination complaints must occur, so check with your EEOC office and act quickly. The first step in the process is an attempt to reach an informal resolution or "adjustment." If the adjustment is not made, you will be advised of your right to a hearing or a decision without a hearing. If you ask for a hearing and are not satisfied with the results, an appeal can be made to the EEOC Office of Review and Appeals, and/or you can file a civil suit with the Federal District Court. Opportunity is provided for a complainant to choose a representative at every level of the processing of a complaint. (Similar hierarchical approaches to dealing with on-the-job discrimination should be available and fully described in policy manuals.) Obviously, following EEOC procedures is a lengthy process which understandably discourages many people, but it is important to realize that you do have some legal recourse.

ISOLATION

A last serious problem confronting the Black woman professional is isolation. Being constantly viewed as a representative of Black women and enduring others' discomfort are lonely challenges. I have found it helpful to join both minority and female professional groups in order to build a network of people who are able to validate my experiences and who are not too threatened to acknowledge and openly discuss the existence and prevalence of discriminatory practices. Both the American Historical Association and the American Psychological Association's Psychology of Women Division has a section for Black women (addresses are given in Appendix). Similar organizations at regional and local levels can boost morale for Black women professionals who might otherwise experience intense isolation.

The pressures on you are at times likely to erode your self-esteem. To bolster your spirits during discouraging times of having to repeatedly prove yourself to others, review your accomplishments privately to maintain an accurate self-perception. This can be done easily by keeping a copy of your updated resume beside your bed or under your pillow.

As a Black woman professional, the racist and sexist barriers which you might encounter will be very stressful. Be sure to pursue support as well as relaxing activities away from the job. Join interest groups with foci other than your work, but limit your involvement so that you don't burn out. Spiritual activities can lead to supportive friendships. Be prepared to attend activities alone, especially if you are single and your job is in an area that isolates you from your friends and family. Take time to rest. Plan to sleep late at least one weekend morning each month. Find a good restaurant with decent service and become a good customer. Get an answering machine that allows screening of calls. If at all possible, try to find a job within an hour's driving distance of a city which offers a choice of activities.

In some job situations, there is no way to make your position comfortable. Under such circumstances, it is wise to keep your options open in terms of finding alternate employment. When looking for a new job, outside support from other professionals is essential — advertising your plans at work could lead to increased discomfort on the job. Maximize the regions, as well as the types of positions, in which you are willing to seek employment. Keep your personal goals in mind, and consider your present (and, if necessary, your next) position as a stepping stone to something better.

The survival tactics in this chapter have been useful for me both professionally and personally. I have found it essential to maintain a focus on my achievement and potential while innocuously breaking down the barriers which interfere with the fulfillment of my job duties.

■ 12
Issues Confronting Lesbian Academics

JOANNA BUNKER ROHRBAUGH

The unique problems of lesbian academics stem from continuing discrimination and intolerance. This chapter will briefly consider some of the problems caused by being forced to hide one's sexual preference, and then go on to discuss a variety of coping strategies which can help with these difficulties.

It is no longer fashionable to persecute lesbians, at least not in liberal academic communities. Lesbians have not been officially "sick" since 1973, when the American Psychiatric Association removed homosexuality from its list of psychiatric disorders. Despite this "instant cure," however, things have not changed dramatically. In the academic world — as well as in other professional settings — one's personality is considered crucial to competence and success. And the personality prescribed for all women is a heterosexual one. Some of our colleagues now profess to "know a nice lesbian" or, even more likely, "a nice gay couple." This does not prevent them from discriminating against us, however. The forms of this discrimination have simply become less blatant.

All of us are familiar with the anxiety caused by having to deal with others' feelings about our lesbianism. Since women are always assumed to be heterosexual in this society, we must always ask ourselves whether someone knows we are lesbian, whether we want them to know, and how we should tell them. We cannot escape from these questions and interactions; even the most open lesbian is repeatedly assumed to be straight, and must decide, each time, whether it is worth the energy to correct that assumption.

Many of us cannot afford to be open at work. Yet the constant worry of being discovered can rob the closeted lesbian of spontaneity and distract her from creative endeavors. While other academics are concentrating on the study being discussed, we may find ourselves analyzing a gesture, look, or phrase which could indicate knowledge of and hostility toward our lesbianism. I often think of the woman professional waiting to give a speech; as she is introduced she is thinking about how she must buy toilet paper on the way home. The lesbian in that situation may have to think not only about toilet paper, but also about how to manage the social interactions at the party following her speech, where she will have to justify her lack of a male escort, once again.

Closeted lesbians often cope with these pressures by maintaining a lesbian and feminist reference group outside of the work place. This group may be small, made up of close friends and acquaintances, or it may be larger, with a political focus. Feminist political groups are an excellent source of personal support, as most of you already know. When I think back over my years in training, I cannot imagine how I would have made it without the various political groups with which I worked. With them I could be myself, could appear with my lover and be treated as someone with a full personal and social life. In my first years in graduate school, I would race across town each afternoon in order to do some feminist "shit work" and eat dinner with my friends and co-workers. Heartened by our shared humor and vision of life, I would return to my academic office in the evening. As the years have gone by, my routine and method of keeping in touch have varied. Always, however, I have arranged regular work meetings, dinner meetings, hanging-out times: times of acceptance, oases of political sanity in the male-oriented and homophobic academic world.

Another tried and true coping method is to develop a network of lesbians in similar academic programs or professional jobs. Lesbians who work on the same campus or in the same company may have dinner together periodically, for instance, just to touch base. This is the simplest way to develop a supportive network, since it requires only that you be able to identify yourselves to each other. Having done this, you can meet discreetly without making any public announcements or doing any advertising.

Other networks are somewhat more public, and hence involve a slightly greater risk for closeted lesbians. Academics and professionals in similar fields may want to form discussion groups similar to the ones run by the Gay Academic Union. In Boston a few years ago, the now defunct Lesbian Academic Union met once a month to discuss intellectual topics. One of the members would be invited to present a colloquium, which was followed by an informal reception. Announcements were placed in local papers, and a confidential mailing list was used for flyers.

Broader networks may involve lesbians throughout a metropolitan area. One such group was organized in Boston seven or eight years ago by a handful of lesbian academics. They named the group the Gay Professional Women's Group and invited all lesbian professionals to join in discussions and socializing. A few discreet announcements were placed in the local gay and feminist papers; no further publicity was required. The group has grown to over 200 members from a wide variety of professional, academic, and business careers. We meet once a month to socialize and hear presentations about various practical and intellectual topics, and have seasonal parties and occasional day-long outings. Although the very success of the group has ended the intimacy of the original, small gatherings, it is invigorating and reassuring to look over this sea of blazers and realize that there are this many lesbians in local professions. None of us is ever too secure to benefit from such periodic confirmation of our life styles and identities.

While attending such a group, however, one often runs into students, colleagues, staff, and others from one's work life. This prospect keeps many lesbians from appearing at any public gathering; some are closeted and fear exposure, while others are more open about being lesbian but fear the discomfort of such social encounters. The restricted social institutions available to lesbians make such incidents inevitable for a socially active lesbian professional and underscore the importance of clarifying one's professional role. All professional women face the dilemma of delineating their differences from support staff and other women in the work place. As feminists, we feel a sense of solidarity with women in other job categories and ranks; as professionals, we are expected to keep our distance in order to maintain an appropriately cool and authoritative demeanor. Each woman must find her own resolution, her own way to nourish feminist bonds with other women while retaining her identity as a competent, if not distant, supervisor and professional.

Such role clarification is especially crucial for the lesbian professional because of the complexities of sharing a stigmatized and sometimes secret identity with those over whom we have authority. This point was brought home to me in a dramatic way several years ago, when I was teaching. At the time I was open about my lesbianism with individual students, but I did not make any public pronouncements in class. I felt that my job would be endangered by public statements, and that the statements would also make some students unnecessarily uncomfortable. Those who needed to know about my lesbianism often approached me privately; this discreet way of providing an available role-model was comfortable for me. My discretion enraged the vocal lesbians in the class, however, who accused me of being old-fashioned, conservative, and scared. They felt that times had changed, that there was no great risk in being open in an academic setting; they felt that people in powerful positions such as mine had an obligation to be "out," to provide positive role-models for younger and less fortunate lesbians. I understood their logic; they understood mine. We continued to disagree. In the classroom, they would bait me about lesbianism in an apparent effort to force me to change my position.

These women shared a secret about me, as would a psychotherapy client, employee, or co-worker who ran into a closeted lesbian in a bar or other social setting. In dealing with them, I had to maintain my professorial stance while simultaneously affirming our common politics and lesbian identities. I was the professional responsible for the classroom; I continued to follow my own conscience and to assert my authority to run the discussions and assign grades. The clash with these students made me anxious, however, and caused me to reevaluate my teaching style and stance of quasi-openness about my lesbianism. Such reevaluations are inevitable; they can be especially growth-enhancing if we have already given some thought to our position within the professional, feminist, and lesbian communities.

This incident also illustrates the importance of preparing ourselves for the time when we will be asked about our lesbianism. Every lesbian, no matter how closeted, has had the experience of someone asking direct or oblique questions about her life style. What will she say? One possibility is to develop the expertise to turn these inquiries aside with a light or joking comment.

"You're always here alone," an inebriated department chairman said to a friend of mine at a reception. "What are you, a dyke?"

Covering her panic, this woman (who was a lesbian experienced at non-confrontational avoidance) replied, "Oh Donald, you're so outrageous. You know that I come alone to enjoy your company. I talk with everyone more when I'm by myself." She smiled, sipped her drink, and moved off to get another olive.

Other encounters permit a less controlled response. After my first day in a clinical setting, for example, I spent the evening relaxing at a local lesbian bar. As one of my friends was teaching me the "bump" in the middle of an empty dance floor, my most difficult new client walked in. She lingered near the door just long enough to be sure that I had seen her, then fled. This client was frequently psychotic and always emotionally unstable; in fact, I found out later that she was assigned to me as a test of the new "Harvard feminist" on the staff. What to do when I saw her again in a few days? If I denied my lesbianism, what would it do to her already tenuous reality-testing? (Not to mention what such a denial would do to my self-respect and our mutual trust.) On the other hand, what would the client do with this information? As someone notorious for clinic-shopping and emergency visits throughout the metropolitan mental health system, would she try to manipulate or embarrass me during one of her fits of anger?

I had not expected to be faced with this dilemma quite so soon, or so dramatically. I decided to acknowledge the incident, but to treat it in as matter-of-fact a manner as possible (given the circumstances). I felt that the client's well-being was more important than my discomfort and that our relationship had to be based on directness and honesty. If I could not admit my own lesbianism, I thought, how could I expect to help the client deal with hers?

Each of us has to make her own decisions about how to handle such encounters. It is wise to expect the unexpected, however, and to try to plan your response. How would you feel if you met a client, student, employee, or co-worker in a lesbian setting or at a women's concert when you were with your lover and "dykey" friends? Rehearsing your response, even if only mentally, can be a great help in resolving some of the conflicts surrounding these situations. Try to decide how much disclosure you could tolerate, in which situations, and with whom. Consider the consequences and be prepared to face them. In doing this, you need to separate your fears from your realistic expectations. Most situations are not as dramatic as the one I have described here, yet they all share the common element of involuntary disclosure of private information. A sense of intrusion is perhaps inevitable, but need not be overwhelming. Once one or two such incidents have been weathered successfully, the feeling of threat diminishes.

Another way to cope with the threat of disclosure is to take the initiative: tell people yourself. Of course, not everyone is receptive to this information, so that most lesbians choose to discuss their life style with only a trusted few. In a work setting, it is very important to have at least one person with whom you can be yourself, your whole self. This person can give you a sense of support and can also serve as a confidante. Just knowing that she or he is there, and that she or he likes and respects you, can be very helpful in maintaining your perspective and sense of humor in the face of the subtle hostilities which often accompany homophobia.

In addition to such individual allies, you may want to seek out more organized support. A number of lesbian psychologists, for instance, have found essential support in professional organizations. (See Appendix for a listing of relevant organizations.) Many lesbian academics have found it helpful to affiliate themselves with the Women's Studies program; here they can make collegial friends in a more relaxed and open atmosphere, without fearing reprisals for their life style. Other lesbians who work in unionized settings have found the women's caucuses to be very helpful, both in their own work place and in a broader setting such as the state or national organization. Feminist groups within various academic disciplines are also a great source of support as well as intellectual excitement; lesbian psychologists who belong to the Association for Women in Psychology and Division 35 (Psychology of Women) of APA can certainly attest to this.

In closing, I would like to emphasize that regardless of the particular coping strategies you choose, it is essential to follow your own leanings. And remember that it is important to unite with other feminists. Since all women exist outside the male establishment, it is crucial that we maintain a sense of community. I often think of a friend of mine who earned her Master's degree, only to discover that she was not treated with respect. So she got her Ph.D., only to discover that she was still not taken seriously. Desperate, she contemplated changing fields, getting a medical degree, so that then, surely then, she would *be somebody*. What she gradually realized was that no list of academic credentials, however impressive, will ever make women invulnerable to sexism. We must develop a sense of strength and community as women, with new norms for the process of conducting our lives and our work. These norms must be inclusive rather than exclusive, norms which permit each of us to live our lives openly, proudly, and according to our individual conscience and politics.

■ three
ALTERNATIVES TO ACADEME

■ 13
Starting a Private Therapy Practice

LINDA GARNETS

The decision to begin the independent practice of psychotherapy raises several important issues for the woman therapist. Private practice means "being on your own" in the delivery of clinical services; that is, it means creating your own structure and becoming your own "boss." The transition from training experiences or agency work to independent practice requires careful planning, which should include developing objectives for private practice, deciding on office arrangements, building a practice, determining the therapeutic structure, considering ethical and legal issues, and becoming self-employed. In this chapter, I will discuss issues for women mental health care professionals to consider and strategies to use in handling the transition into private clinical practice.

Issues for starting a private practice are similar for women and men. However, the traditional sex-role socialization process as well as cultural expectations of women may lead some women starting in private practice to feel strain in the new role. For example, research has shown that women are socialized to depend on feedback from others for their self-esteem. But private practice does not include a formal structure for supervision or interaction with peers to provide that feedback. Also, prevailing social expectations assume that men play instrumental roles while women play expressive ones. "Expressive" women in mental health fields need to deal with the "instrumental" aspects of conducting a business when they enter a private practice.

Even with these considerations, it is a good time for women psychologists, psychiatrists, social workers, and counselors to be embarking on private practice. Not long ago in the mental health fields, male practitioners were preferentially sought by clients because people generally viewed men as experts and authorities. Now both sexes are increasingly seeking women therapists. In addition, there is more support for women to enter this profession. Owing to the impact of the women's movement, committees and groups throughout the mental health professions have been organized around the concerns of women therapists and clients. As a result, professional networks of women exist in most related fields, providing a "community" for women practitioners.

PRIVATE PRACTICE OBJECTIVES

In starting a private practice, you need to plan how best to set up your work. First, you should clarify your objectives — what kind of a practice would you like to have? Specific questions to ask yourself include: Why do you want to start a private practice now? What are your short-term (one-year) and long-term (five-year) plans for this practice? With what kinds of clients do you wish to work (age, gender, race, type of problem)? What particular specialty areas, if any, do you wish to emphasize in your clinical work — older adults, incest survivors, eating disorders, or others? Are you aiming toward a full- or part-time practice? If part-time, what else would you like to do? How much of your total income do you wish to earn from the practice? Do you prefer working alone or do you want access to other colleagues where you work? How does your interest in being a psychotherapist fit with your personal commitments to your profession, your community, and your other interests?

Answering these questions for yourself can provide the foundation for a plan which will guide the many practical decisions you need to make. You should base your answers on your own interests, expertise, and life circumstances. For example, if you wish to focus your practice on older adults, you may build into your outreach some case consultation to Senior Citizen Centers. It also would be wise to find office space with few stairs which is within walking distance from these programs or near bus lines. As this example illustrates, once you have clarified your objectives, you can concentrate your efforts on choosing a setting and promotion plan which furthers these aims.

OFFICE ARRANGEMENTS

Once you have identified for yourself the kind of practice you would like to have, you will be ready to consider the kind of office space arrangement which would best suit you. To decide on office space, consider the following four factors: Do you want to sublet, lease, or own your office or work out of your home? What would be a good geographic location for you? Do you want a solo practice, a partnership, a shared space with others, or a group practice? What type of physical features do you need in your office, given your client population? To guide your decisions about office space, consider your own goals, preferences, and work-style needs. The pros and cons of choosing various arrangements are discussed below.

Sublet, Lease, Buy, or Home Office

Sublet space generally is rented by the hour or by blocks of time (e.g., half-day or full-day rates). It can be a useful initial arrangement for your practice. Subletting a space has the advantage of allowing you some control over how much money you spend, of giving you the chance to start independent practice without making too large a commitment of time and money, and of putting you in contact with at least one colleague, from whom you rent. On the other hand, subletting space may place limitations both on your ability to expand your practice and on your flexibility with clients in setting up appointment times. Also, subletting gives you very limited control over office furnishings, if any, and your name may not be included in building listings. The fact that the space is not "yours" can sometimes be difficult psychologically for women clinicians who are trying to establish their own identity as independent practitioners. In contrast, clinicians who lease their own space from the outset have the advantage of having greater flexibility of time and of feeling a sense of ownership; however, they often experience the financial burdens of matching costs with income.

If you decide to sublet as a first step, consider the possibilities within the space or suite for later expansion. Otherwise, you need to be prepared for the possibility of having to move to a different office suite when you are ready to lease space.

Buying office space has many tax benefits and, if financially possible, should be considered by those who plan to have a full-time practice and are interested in managing property.

In deciding whether or not to create an office in your home, you need to balance the greater convenience and cost-effectiveness of this arrangement with issues such as safety (since clients will know where you live), privacy (for yourself, your clients, and your household), zoning regulations regarding businesses in residential areas, and role boundaries (the clinical and practical impact of not separating work from home).

Geographic Location

In determining office location, consider its accessibility both for your clients and for yourself. The following questions may help guide your deliberations. What are the zoning regulations in the area regarding the practice of therapy? Where is the office located in relation to major routes? What are the traffic patterns like near the office at the day or evening times you wish to work? If possible, you want to select a location that maximizes the opportunities for clients to reach you relatively easily from diverse parts of the city or town in which you practice. Is there available, convenient, free, or low-cost parking around the office? How convenient is the office to your other professional and personal responsibilities? Is it located near the potential populations with which you wish to work? Try to choose an area that will not have too much noise, and which will be safe for clients who come both during the day and at night.

Solo Practice, Partnership, Shared Space, or Group Practice

In deciding the kind of practice you want, think about whether working alone or in association with others best suits your personal work style. In starting out, many women therapists find it helpful to establish contact and to enhance referral opportunities by setting up their offices within an existing group practice or in a suite of offices with other therapists. This allows costs to be shared among suite members and provides support, referrals, and the benefits of an established group. Compared to a solo practice, shared space has the potential drawback of making it harder to establish a name apart from the group. Clients' sense of privacy also may be reduced, since in group practice, clients generally share a common waiting area. However, a solo practice may be more costly and isolating.

If you do want to share a suite with one or more therapists, find out as much as you can about your compatibility with the other clinicians.

For example, a colleague of mine, whose theoretical orientation is psychodynamic, sublet an office in a suite of Gestalt therapists. As a result, she found that her referrals were affected by people assuming that she, too, was a Gestalt therapist. Also, some of the techniques used by the other therapists required loud exercises, which interfered with her own therapy sessions.

If you are interested in joining a partnership or group practice, find out the nature of their legal contract, the kinds of clients they see, the theoretical orientations they use, their years of experience working together, and the areas of expertise of the members. In addition, talk with other colleagues and community members about the reputation and perceived expertise of the partnership or group. Based on this information, decide on how compatible you are with the aims and structure of the partnership or group.

Physical Features

In selecting a suitable office space for yourself and your clients, consider the physical features of the office and building which could affect your work. For example, how well soundproofed are the offices? Does the office have a separate entrance and exit to minimize the chance of clients seeing each other? Where are the bathrooms located in the building and how accessible are they for the population working with you? Is the building wheelchair-accessible? If you do family or group work, is the room large enough? It is also important to check lighting, heating, air conditioning, and other aspects of a comfortable physical environment. It helps to keep in mind that you may spend hours at a time in one closed room.

BUILDING YOUR PRACTICE: BECOMING KNOWN

Although you may be changing the arena of your work by developing a private practice, the commitment to your profession and community probably won't change. In developing your clientele, you also are developing new ways to serve your community. There are several approaches you can use simultaneously to develop a clientele: establish professional and community referral networks, present seminars and workshops to professional and community groups, and build contacts through professional affiliations.

To establish professional and community referral networks, send announcements to other clinicians you know at mental health agencies, to other private practitioners, and to any organization, agency, or business that potentially may refer clients to you (e.g., lawyers, doctors, police departments). Follow these announcements with personal phone calls to colleagues who are familiar with your work and who are well-established in the clinical community. These contacts should be used to assist you in getting onto agency referral lists, as well as to provide a referral base for your practice. A related strategy involves advertising in newsletters and newspapers that target the population you are interested in serving. List your areas of expertise in your advertising and on your business cards.

Offering seminars and workshops on mental health–related issues to both the professional community and the general public can fill an important community need while helping you professionally. For example, if you are interested in working with children and families, you can volunteer to provide a seminar on child development to the local parent–teacher association, local community center, YWCA, church group, or NOW chapter. Other groups may be reached by offering continuing education workshops at local community colleges or universities.

To identify workshop opportunities, check your local newspapers for agencies and community organizations that offer training and public education. A colleague of mine once noticed a public service announcement in the newpaper about a single women's group being formed at a local YWCA. Because of her concern for single mothers, she called and offered to be a guest speaker at one of their meetings. She subsequently became involved with the YWCA program and was listed on their referral network.

Similarly, you may consider providing services (either paid or voluntary) to mental health clinics or to graduate training programs. Possibilities here include supervision or consultation to staff and students.

To build and strengthen professional affiliations, develop a network of other therapists working with populations similar to your own. Subscribe to local, city, county, or state clinical and mental health newsletters in your field to keep abreast of relevant information within your specialty. Attend professional events to meet other clinicians and build a collegial network.

An important set of networks to tap are the women's and feminist professional groups. This will put you in contact with professional women in related fields, such as law and medicine, who may be referral sources.

Contact the regional coordinators of the national association in your field; they may be able to line you up with other feminist therapists or professional activities in your area. (The addresses of the national associations of psychiatry, psychology, social work, and marriage and family counselors are listed in the Appendix.)

I personally have found joining professional associations to be a very effective way to develop contacts. When I first moved to Los Angeles, I contacted a group of women professionals planning a national conference of the Association for Women in Psychology. I wanted to be part of an active organization concerned with issues in women's mental health. I joined the conference planning committee, which enabled me to make a great many contacts, as well as to learn more about the feminist psychological community. After the national conference, a regional group was formed, which has continued to meet on a bimonthly basis for the past five years. The meetings are structured to allow time both for networking and for members to exchange information about women and psychology. This experience greatly enhanced the rate at which I was able to integrate myself into the women's psychology community in Los Angeles.

One final point about building your practice — it takes time. Plan a strategy which includes consideration of how you will support yourself until the practice pays for itself.

THERAPEUTIC STRUCTURE

Certain professional issues come up as you enter independent practice. Your livelihood is more closely linked to treatment decisions. You are now the one in charge of setting up the conditions of your working relationship directly with clients. Unlike agency work, how the clinical hour and fees are structured is more under your control. Beginning private practitioners often experience anxiety and stress about these issues.

Starting practitioners must set clear policies about fees and time. In setting and maintaining fees, it is helpful to talk with other therapists to find out how they operate and how they handle the myriad ways clients test the boundaries of fee arrangements. Fees vary greatly by discipline, experience, and what the market will bear (ranging from $40 to over $100 a session). For instance, beginning licensed Ph.D.s in psychology will be able to charge more than beginning social workers. In setting fees, determine your rates by finding out the going rates other therapists in your field with similar experience charge. Also take into account the minimum needed to cover your expected office expenses.

You also will have to decide whether you want clients to pay at each session or on a monthly basis, your policy concerning insurance reimbursements, and how to treat missed sessions. There are two routes to consider concerning insurance reimbursements: either clients pay you in full and then get reimbursed by the insurance company, or clients pay their portion of the bill and you get reimbursed from the insurance company. Regarding missed sessions, policies vary greatly. Some clinicians charge for every session, whether the client comes or not, whereas others charge if the client does not cancel the appointment 24 or 48 hours in advance. Yet others do not charge for a canceled session if it is rescheduled during the same week.

Private practitioners differ on how they charge fees for the intitial consultation session. Therapists concerned with the client as "consumer" value the opportunity for prospective clients to "shop around" for a therapist, and charge nothing or have a reduced fee for the initial session. Other therapists view the first session as providing the client with assistance in understanding problems and charge their regular or a higher fee.

Various policies are followed by independent practitioners regarding reduced fees. Many therapists are concerned with providing quality services to individuals from different socioeconomic backgrounds. Some set a full fee, and then offer a certain number of low-fee slots. Another strategy is to set up a fee range to include lower amounts, or to set a full fee and then offer a certain number of no-fee slots.

Making decisions about how often to see clients and the length of sessions are based on clients' needs and therapeutic orientation. The important consideration here is that whatever decisions are made about frequency and length of sessions, conscientious efforts to be consistent must be made. Sometimes therapists beginning in private practice have difficulty adhering to the boundaries they have established because of their discomfort about being in business for themselves. Examine your own attitudes and values about these issues and talk to colleagues to discover how they approach this professional dilemma.

An illustration of this conflict occurred for a therapist friend of mine. After deciding the overall number and times of hours she wished to work, she found herself frequently and unhappily adjusting her schedule to accommodate her clients' requests. During discussions with a group of colleagues, she discovered that she felt that she was charging too much for her services. Her fear of losing clients affected her ability to deal directly with clinical issues for clients who changed appointments frequently.

There is no "correct" formula for handling structural issues in therapy. What is important is to decide on the parameters for your practice, and then to be firm in holding to that framework. It is common practice to reevaluate these arrangements for yourself periodically as your practice develops, and as your identity as a clinician solidifies with more experience.

ETHICAL AND LEGAL CONSIDERATIONS

Before starting your practice, it is imperative that you familiarize yourself with ethical and legal guidelines for private practice, including the ethical standards of your professional field, current state laws and regulations regarding practice, guidelines of your State Licensing Bureau, community resources dealing with hospitalization, and specialized mental health services. Knowledge of laws regarding dangerousness, hospitalization, child-abuse reporting, confidentiality, and professional liability is particularly important.

You will need to know where and when to refer clients for alternative helping resources, including peer self-help groups (e.g., Alcoholics Anonymous or Parents Without Partners); crisis intervention systems (e.g., for drug and alcohol abuse, violence against women and children, suicide, and pregnancy or abortion); psychiatric hospitals; and agencies and private practitioners who offer low fees. Decide how you will handle clients who need medication. Many therapists have an arrangement with a nearby hospital or psychiatrist to prescribe medication; others try to set up a suite which includes a psychiatrist on site. Locate any hospitals in the area that permit psychologists or social workers, as well as psychiatrists, to have admitting and treatment privileges.

In terms of ethical considerations, the feminist mental health community provides some valuable perspectives on maintaining an ethical, nonsexist practice. As Hare-Mustin, Marecek, Kaplan, and Liss-Levinson (1979) state in "Rights of Clients, Responsibilities of Therapists:"

> Historically, ethical codes for therapists were drawn up to protect the professions from regulation by external agencies. Implicit in the ethical codes,

however, is a model for the client-therapist relationship that fosters the goals of mental health. . . . Therapists need to take responsibility for incorporating ethical standards into their practices so that clients' rights will be an integral part of therapy (p. 3).

There are four ethical dilemmas to which you may particularly want to attend as you start out in private practice. The first concerns the dilemma of trying to work within the limits of your own competence, while at the same time trying to recruit clients to build your practice. Many people find it difficult when starting out to refer any potential client to another therapist, even if the problems the client presents are outside the therapist's expertise. Consequently, these therapists may find themselves "over their heads" on a case, without the backup of an agency.

This occurred to an acquaintance of mine, who had a battered woman as a client. This therapist had heard a few lectures dealing with domestic violence, but had never worked with any clients. She decided to see the client, only to find herself overwhelmed with clinical and safety management issues for her client.

One strategy to reduce the likelihood of experiencing this type of dilemma is to list for yourself the kinds of clients with whom you currently are qualified to work, and those you are not. Then draw up a list of other practitioners and agencies to whom you can refer clients who are outside your level of expertise. Decide whether you can handle the amount of case management the client will require, given the clients you already have. Drug-addicted, suicidal, or borderline personality clients may require considerable time commitment. Assess your limits.

A second issue arises because the therapist relies directly on clients for her livelihood when in private practice. Decisions regarding what is in the client's best interest may be influenced by the therapist's economic need to keep clients. For example, a woman sought help from a therapist I know to cope with the loss of a parent. After the crisis had subsided, the therapist thought the client should continue to deal with underlying issues involving autonomy and loss which had emerged during the crisis intervention. The client was not interested in pursuing therapy further. Upon self-examination, the therapist realized that she was inappropriately invested in the client's continuing because of her anxiety about the stability of her income.

In order to handle the general tension between providing service and running a business, set up a time line for building your practice so that each client does not become "the one" you need to pay your bills.

A third ethical issue concerns ways to avoid creating dual, multiple, or overlapping roles with clients which can dilute or contaminate the therapeutic relationship. In building a practice, many therapists recruit potential clients by relying on personal and professional contacts among their closest friends and colleagues. This sometimes leads clinicians to accept as clients acquaintances, colleagues, friends of clients, and other people with whom they come in contact in other roles they perform, such as teaching, or political or recreational activities. This situation can be especially problematic for clinicians who specialize in women's, feminist, or lesbian issues which might bring them into substantial contact with their clients outside the office.

The problem of overlapping roles can be illustrated by a few examples. In one case, a woman therapist I know began seeing the depressed wife of a colleague. During the course of treatment, the therapist learned of disturbing aspects of the husband's behavior which affected both the therapy and the collegial relationship. In another case, a therapist accepted into treatment a friend of a client she currently was seeing. The friends subsequently became lovers, which created a complicated set of therapeutic and confidentiality issues for the therapist. In a third situation, a feminist therapist was referred to a client who was looking for someone who specialized in working with incest survivors. Both the therapist and the client were active in the sexual-assault-prevention movement and frequently crossed paths at political meetings. This overlap created problems for the client in therapy.

To avoid the problems associated with role overlap, try to minimize the number of people you see who come from the same friendship network or work or political setting, or from you own network.

A fourth ethical issue in clinical practice concerns maintaining one's objectivity in work with clients. Countertransference and professional "blindspots" which may lead to loss of objectivity are natural aspects of therapy. Private practice can be an isolating, intense, and emotionally charged professional activity which therapists cannot freely discuss with their friends and family. Yet without some avenue to discuss issues raised by doing therapy, a clinician risks the danger of putting her own needs above those of her clients, or of reenacting issues with clients, rather than resolving them.

There are several strategies to handle general clinical and countertransference issues. A typical one is to set up clinical consultation (paid or collaborative) with another psychotherapist or a group of colleagues for either case conferencing or to provide ongoing feedback in maintaining objectivity. In setting up such an arrangement, plan ways to protect the confidentiality of clients by selecting a consultation group whose clients are not likely to overlap with your clients' networks.

Other strategies are just to talk to more established women practitioners to find out how they approach this dilemma, or to seek psychotherapy for yourself. It is also helpful to take advantage of continuing education opportunities to increase your knowledge and to use as a forum to discuss these concerns, and to participate in professional associations where these issues are discussed.

Some of the dilemmas described above can be avoided by using the initial interview as a screening tool to decide whether or not to work with a given client. Some clinicians prefer to do sufficient screening on the telephone, discussing fee, time, referral source, presenting problem, and so on. Others prefer to use the verbal and nonverbal data gathered from a face-to-face interview to make this determination. Questions to ask yourself include: Are the person's problems within my area of expertise and competence? Is there any way that I can foresee that work with this client will create a dual relationship or conflict of interest? Do I experience any strong countertransference reactions to this client regarding values or personality that may limit my objectivity when working with her or him? Another strategy to minimize confusion of roles is to use the first session to explain the goals, expectations, risks, rights, and boundaries associated with services.

BUSINESS STATUS: SELF-EMPLOYED

Finally, independent practice requires a change in your professional status to that of self-employed. In order to manage this change and to protect yourself professionally, you need to take a number of steps.

Recordkeeping

First, you need to maintain sets of records for legal, clinical, and tax purposes. In an atmosphere of increasing malpractice suits in the mental health field, it is particularly important to keep accurate client records in accord with licensing and professional guidelines. Consult a lawyer who has worked with mental health professionals, your professional association, and colleagues to determine what recordkeeping system would best document that you are providing a client with an "acceptable level of care." Keep all such records confidential in a locked file drawer.

Second, you need to adopt a system of recording to document your professional expenses for tax purposes. These records should include all allowable professional expenses such as consultation, entertainment, office equipment and supplies, books and journals, utilities, furnishings for your office, copying, postage, telephone and answering services, office space, parking, conferences, outside services (e.g., accounting, legal), advertising, professional dues, education and seminars, licenses and permits, and malpractice insurance. Generally, therapists keep a daily register in which they tally all professional expenses. Record books are easily available in business supply stores. You also need to keep detailed records of your mileage and travel expenses, including date, purpose, and mileage. The precise way to record these data changes each year as the tax laws are adjusted, so it is important to consult an accountant.

Billing

It is crucial to keep accurate, up-to-date records of fees collected from each client. These records serve as the basis for computing your annual income. The records minimally should include dates of sessions, type of service provided (individual, couple, group, family, or evaluation), fee charged, payment received from client, and payment received from insurance companies. Keep copies of all correspondence you have with insurance companies. It is common practice to provide clients with a monthly billing statement, even if fees are collected for each session.

Insurance and Pension Plans

As a self-employed businesswoman, you must make your own provisions for insurance and retirement. Consult an insurance agent and also look into plans offered through professional associations. Generally, most clinicians in full-time private practice need the following type of insurance coverage: malpractice, disability, office overhead, and major medical. The Internal Revenue Service allows tax deferment on three types of retirement accounts: Individual Retirement Accounts (IRA), for up to $2,000 a year; a SEP-IRA (Simplified Employee Pension), which entitles you to save up to 15% or $30,000 during one taxable year; and Keogh accounts, limited to a maximum contribution of the lesser of $30,000 or 25% of compensation during a single year.

Business License

You may be required to pay an annual fee to operate a business in the town or city in which you work. To obtain this business license, contact the governmental office within the area you are practicing. Fees are based on your gross income from the previous fiscal year.

Office Expenses

You should expect initially to purchase the following: office space, utilities, supplies (e.g., cards, stationery, billing and recordkeeping forms), a telephone answering service, and equipment (e.g., telephone, typewriter or word processor).

Some clinicians prefer to use a 24-hour answering service, while others like an answering machine. The advantages of the answering service are that clients have contact with another person and that it has 24-hour capabilities for handling emergencies by cross-connecting to your current location. However, answering services can be inconsistent in the quality of service depending on the operator on duty. In addition, they may make mistakes in obtaining accurate information, such as correct telephone numbers. On the other hand, although answering machines are less personal, they maintain client's privacy better, clients can leave as long a message as they wish, and the therapist can hear how the client sounds to determine the urgency of the call. To handle emergencies, therapists with answering machines sometimes have clients use a pager for crises only.

CONCLUSION

The key to success in starting your private practice is planning. Thinking through your ideas, setting goals, and considering the professional and practical issues you face will prepare you well for the challenges and demands of independent practice.

USEFUL REFERENCES FOR STARTING A PRIVATE PRACTICE

American Psychiatric Association. (1973). The principles of medical ethics with annotations especially applicable to psychiatry. *American Journal of Psychiatry, 130,* 1057–1064.

American Psychological Association. (1977). *Ethical standards of psychologists* (rev. ed.). Washington, DC: Author.

American Psychological Association. (1977). *Standards for providers of psychological services* (rev. ed.). Washington, DC: Author.

Berman, A.L., & Cohen-Sandler, R. (1983). Suicide and malpractice: Expert testimony and the standard of care. *Professional Psychology: Research and Practice, 1,* 6–19.

Borenzweig, H. (1981). Agency vs. private practice: Similarities and differences. *Social Work, 26,* 239–244.

Brodsky, A.M., & Hare-Mustin, R. (1980). *Women and psychotherapy: An assessment of research and practice.* New York: Guilford Press.

Campion, T.F., & Peck, J.A. (1979). Ingredients of a psychiatric malpractice law suit. *Psychiatric Quarterly, 5,* 236–241.

Cohen, R.J. (1979). *Malpractice: A guide for mental health professionals.* New York: Free Press.

Coyne, J.C. (1976). The place of informed consent in ethical dilemmas. *Journal of Consulting and Clinical Psychology, 44,* 1015–1016.

Eberlein, L. (1977). Counselors beware! Clients have rights. *Personnel and Guidance Journal, 56,* 219–223.

Gabriel, E. (1977). The private practice of social work. In *Encyclopedia of Social Work.* Washington, DC: National Association of Social Workers.

Haas, L.J., Fennimore, D., & Warburton, J. (1983). A bibliography on ethical and legal issues in psychotherapy, 1970–1982. *Professional Psychology: Research and Practice, 14*(6), 771–779.

Hare, R.T., & Frankena, S.T. (1972). Peer group supervision. *American Journal of Orthopsychiatry, 42,* 527–529.

Hare-Mustin, R. T., Marecek, J., Kaplan, A. G., & Liss-Levinson, N. (1979). Rights of clients, responsibilities of therapists. *American Psychologist, 34,* 3–16.

Hines, P., & Hare-Mustin, R.T. (1978). Ethical concerns in family therapy. *Professional Psychology, 9,* 165–171.

Kaplan, A.G. (1976). Eight stages in the nine-month life span of a feminist therapy training group. *Voices: Journal of the American Academy of Psychotherapists, 12,* 41–45.

Law and Professional Psychology: Special Issue. (1978). *Professional Psychology, 9*(3), 361–525.

National Association of Social Workers. (1967). *Code of ethics.* Washington, DC: Author.

National Association of Social Workers. (1974). *Handbook on the private practice of social work* (rev. ed.). Washington, DC: Author.

Redlich, F., & Mollica, R.F. (1976). Overview: Ethical issues in contemporary psychiatry. *American Journal of Psychiatry, 133,* 125–136.

Rolls, S., & Millen, L. (1981). A guide to violating an injunction in psychotherapy:

On seeing acquaintances as patients. *Psychotherapy: Theory, Research, and Practice, 18*(2), 179–187.

Schulberg, H.C. (1976). Quality-of-care standards and professional norms. *American Journal of Psychiatry, 133,* 1047–1051.

Shah, S. (1978). Dangerousness: A paradigm for exploring some issues in law and psychology. *American Psychologist, 33,* 224–238.

Siegel, M. (1979). Privacy, ethics, and confidentiality. *Professional Psychology, 10,* 249–256.

Sobel, S. (1984). Independent practice in child and adolescent psychotherapy in small communities: Personal and professional issues. *Psychotherapy, 21* (2), 110–117.

Sullivan, F.W. (1977). Peer review and professional ethics. *American Journal of Psychiatry, 134,* 186–188.

Taylor, R.E. (1978). Demythologizing private practice. *Professional Psychology, 9,* 68–70.

Van Hoose, W.H., & Kottler, J.A. (1977). *Ethical and legal issues in counseling and psychotherapy.* San Francisco: Jossey-Bass.

Vatulano, L.A., & Copeland, B.A. (1980). Trends in continuing education and competency demonstration. *Professional Psychology, 11,* 891–897.

Widigor, T.A., & Rorer, L.G. (1984). The responsible psychotherapist. *American Psychologist, 39*(5), 503–515.

■ 14
Changing Career Directions: Life Outside the Academic Mainstream

SHARON TOFFEY SHEPELA[1]

The time to consider the possibility of life outside of the academic mainstream is:

- Right away, even though you think yourself firmly entrenched in academe (it will free you from thinking that academic work is the only thing someone with your mind and degree can do and will help you to become more sophisticated about the politics and acumen you need to survive, in or out of academe).
- When you look at the number and pattern of tenure decisions at your institution and others.
- When you learn of the geometrically decreasing pool of potential college students.
- When you look at the number of academic jobs listed in your professional journals.

[1]My thanks to Carol Berman, M.S., counselor at The Counseling Center of Hartford College for Women, a career counseling and training center for adult women and men, for her extensive consultation on this chapter, and to the entire counseling staff for their feedback on selected portions of the text. Responsibility for the final version is entirely my own. Thanks too to Janet Carson for her lightning fast and virtually error-free typing.

- When you learn of the number of very well-known and respected women scholars who didn't get tenure at their institutions.
- And, on the cheerful side, when you learn that both jobs and salaries on the "outside" are exciting.

THE TRANSITION: VOLUNTARY OR UN

The hardest thing about leaving academe is believing that there is anything else. Those of us with advanced degrees probably have been in school since we were five or six, socialize only with people who have been in school since they were five or six, and haven't the foggiest notion what all those other people in the world do in their jobs. Faced with the possibility/necessity of looking for a job when in my mid-thirties, I quite honestly got stuck when I thought beyond secretarial work (I couldn't type), working in a book store (there were no jobs), or being a check-out clerk in the grocery store (satisfactory only if I could wait on my former colleagues and drive them mad with guilt over what they had done to me). Rejoice! This is just another learning situation and you have been learning all your life. You're a professional learner, and it not only is a useful skill in this situation, you're about to discover it is a marketable one.

Most of what I am about to suggest can be done from the comfort of your existing job, and for many reasons, that is the ideal paradigm. Even though a job search is often described as a full-time job in itself, when conducted from the security of an existing job it carries the benefits of reduced urgency, available resources (letterhead, clerical staff, copy machines, and phone answering services are invaluable), and the legitimacy which accrues from being employed.

However, many of us have found and will find ourselves exploring these options from the pit of unemployment, and that presents additional problems. You will read excellent suggestions on how to cope with unemployment elsewhere in this book (see chapter by Gore). Let me emphasize a few things here. Coping with loss of self-esteem and legitimacy in your own eyes and in those of others will be a big problem, and you'll need to marshall your own resources and those of your friends and colleagues. I started talking about my unemployment publicly at Association for Women in Psychology meetings and was remarkably buoyed both by those who thanked me for verbalizing the problems they thought they suffered alone (even psychologists think that way) and by comments of support and encouragement from people I had never met. Important tasks were found for me to do, and one colleague, in a life-saving gesture which made me feel like a 'real psychologist" again, asked me to be principal investigator on a grant she had already written and was about to submit. Ask for help from your sisters — it will come and will be invaluable.

Finding a job is a task requiring considerable energy, and energy wanes quickly when you "have nothing to do." Support from others, physical exercise, and a plan will help you keep the energy you will need.

INSIDE ACADEME/OUTSIDE THE MAINSTREAM

Part-time jobs are the academy's answer to sweat shops, but they are an increasing phenomenon as institutions try to cut costs, and many of us are (barely) surviving on them. If you want to stay in academe, or keep your hand in, or want the legitimacy the affiliation can offer you as you pursue other options (see the discussion on consulting below), part-time teaching can be the answer. Part-time jobs are rarely advertised. They are often filled through the old boys' or old girls' network, and from the resumes on hand. This presents a good rationale for making sure that all of your friends and acquaintances know that you are looking for a job, and the department chairs at all of the institutions to which you would be willing to travel have your curriculum vitae. This means that a blitz mailing (one to all relevant institutions regardless of whether they have advertised for a position) is advisable for those who are willing to take part-time positions. A word of advice — reference libraries will often have resources which will tell you the name of the department chair at most institutions of higher education. If you can't type 75 individual letters, have your typist prepare the strong cover letter you have written so that she or he can take the offset copies you have made and, using the same typewriter, type in individual inside addresses and salutations. Word processors make this much easier. Use *only* a letter-quality printer and bond stationery. Your cover letter and resume must speak of your professionalism and qualifications. Anything slipshod or tacky will be an excuse to discard your application from among the many which they receive.

It is entirely appropriate to follow up your letter and vita with a very positive phone call of inquiry, indicating your sincere interest in working in that department, and your availablity for a part-time position were that to be open. If the institution is out of your town, say that you will be in the area on such a date or dates and would like to meet briefly with the departmental chair and/or members of the faculty in your area. The more likely your name is to flash positively into mind when Alice learns on August 3 that her Fulbright has come through and her courses are suddenly sans instructor, the more likely you are to be called. And despair not, these calls often do come in August for the Fall semester.

Part-time jobs need not be a dead end. Full-time jobs are (sometimes) filled from the part-time ranks, especially if you have made a point to make your presence positively felt in the department or school. Make sure your colleagues know you. Be there when they are there, if possible negotiate to have an office, or to share one with another part-time faculty member, 'so that you can see students" (do all you can to make sure your office is in the department in which you are teaching so that you don't get lost tucked away in another department), ask to attend departmental meetings and faculty meetings. Report on your progress to the chair or the head of your subsection. They will not know how well you are doing unless you tell them. Make it sound like friendly collegial conversation. Take on some tasks for the department; make yourself useful.

Part-time jobs in small colleges can be an opportunity for you to pick up administrative skills if you take on additional duties, and those skills, especially if they lead to a job title, can lead to administrative positions and more skills, opening up the possibility of management jobs both in and out of academe.

Alicia Becket is a case in point. A victim of the five-year revolving door phenomenon at a large Western university, she contacted all the institutions of higher education within a reasonable commute of her home. One small private institution contacted her to teach a one-semester course in their history department to replace someone on sabbatical leave. The second semester she taught a noncredit course in their adult evening program — a course she had devised and proposed to the director of that program. The following year she repeated the same schedule, with two courses in the evening program, and talked the dean into hiring her to teach a full-year remedial course in American culture and English for foreign students. When the half-time position of director of noncredit courses opened, Alicia applied and got the position, and at the same time was hired by the history department to teach introductory European history on a renewable one-year appointment. She is now, five years later, a full-time employee of the college, director of continuing and adult education, teaching two history courses a year, with an impressive list of administrative and managerial skills on her curriculum vitae.

Even if you cannot or do not want to parlay your part-time position into full-time teaching, or a combination of teaching and administration at that institution, a part-time job which gives you access to secretarial service, a phone, and letterhead can be the legitimate base from which you make your next move.

Consulting

Part-time jobs can be combined with consulting work, a meld which has proven fruitful and exciting for some of our colleagues. In 1985, consultants in training and human resource development were earning $500–$1200/day, more in the applied science and engineering fields. There are several good books on establishing and maintaining a successful, ethical consulting practice. I would recommend *The Profession and Practice of Consultation* (Gallessich, 1982) and *Consultation* (Blake & Moulton, 1983).

Consulting is not easy, and is not for everyone. Still, it can be very rewarding for the right person at the right time. Your personality is critical to the endeavor.

A successful independent consultant must have a good idea *and* be:

- Awesomely self-confident
- Very assertive
- Able to put herself repeatedly into situations into which she has not been invited as she makes "cold" calls on prospective contractors
- A risk taker
- A saleswoman
- Able to take rejection
- Able to work without colleagues
- Independent
- Organized
- Creative
- A problem solver
- An excellent speaker
- Able to handle a group

If you have most of these attributes but not all of them, you have the option of joining forces with someone who has those you lack.

If this list hasn't daunted you, here are a few of the ideas you will find explained in greater detail in the books I mentioned above.

Start small. Don't quit your job and expect to support yourself consulting. Keep or develop an affiliation with an institution of higher education or an established consulting firm. Those affiliations will make you more marketable because you have the prestige and reputation of the institution behind you, and the former can also provide you with some regular income, a remarkably cheering factor when you have gone four months without a contract. Consulting groups will rarely pay you a salary; rather, they offer their name and a desk, phone, and letterhead, those wonderful commodities I've mentioned before.

Spend time looking at what you can sell, and what might be needed out there. Look to your research and writing for those things you know best and are most interested in, and spend the time to develop one program or product. Market just one idea at first; don't go looking for "something in the training area" just because you have been a teacher. There is a world of difference between teaching and training, not the least of which is that you are dealing with adults who will grade *you* on the basis of how much *they* have learned.

Experimental psychologist Marjorie Hale was interested in coping strategies of dual-career couples both personally and professionally. She had researched the topic and had written one article. Her colleague June Goode had written her dissertation on dual-career couples and the two of them were convinced that the information that academicians had gathered on how these couples creatively cope had not filtered to the couples themselves. An idea was born. They began talking about a workshop on creative coping skills for dual-career couples wherever they went, and at a party with several middle managers of a major corporation, got both encouragement and the signal that a proposal for such a workshop would be seriously considered by these people. They contacted a male trainer (if you are working with couples, you'll need a balanced team) Marjorie had seen presenting a program at a local meeting of the American Society for Training and Development (ASTD) and with whom she had been impressed. He agreed to help develop the workshop on a contract that said he would be paid when the workshop was sold to a sponsor (a common arrangement).

Many hours went into the development of the workshop, its focus, goals, exercises, and marketing. The noncredit course division of Marjorie and June's college allowed them to offer an abbreviated form of the workshop for a low fee (they were not paid) in order to test it out and get feedback. They offered another segment of the workshop to students in a graduate business course and their spouses, again for free. The business students were especially helpful in their detailed feedback. It was only after the workshop had been refined through this process, and had been costed out to set a reasonable fee, that the three began marketing it. Their short-term goal was to present the workshops (it had become a series of three short sessions) successfully to one corporate group, so that it could be used as a reference in future marketing efforts.

Some important factors to note in the case study above:

- Trade ideas and program development for future money — this is risk-taking.
- Be willing to try out an idea for free in order to work out the bugs in the system, but don't give so much away that someone else can use your "product" without you.
- Your first corporate job is the hardest to get and the most critical for its reference value.
- Keep your regular job as long as you can. It can take a long time to get a consulting business off the ground.

How do you go about getting that first contract? The same way you get your next job — by using your network. As an academician, you may think you don't know the right people for this task, but you *do*. Let people know you have an exciting product. Your relatives and friends know people who may just know someone who needs what you are selling. All the professionals from whom you buy services, from your hairdresser to your TV service representative, have contacts. Talk about your product and be proud of it.

Have a business card printed. It is not expensive.

Print a classy looking brochure — perhaps one of your friends has access to a laser-printer. They must look professional. One human resource manager said he got 10 proposals across his desk every day and threw most of them away. Don't give him an excuse to throw away yours.

Read books on marketing and sales, or take a marketing course at your local college's evening program.

Join your local chapter of the American Society for Training and Development and go to all their meetings. Listen to everyone and talk about your work.

Join the national ASTD and get their journal and marketing material from hundreds of sources. ASTD mailing lists are a hot commodity.

Getting Institutional Affiliation

If you are unemployed and can't get a part-time job, an institutional affiliation is still important enough to work for. See if you can get an office or research space at a local college or university. It can give you colleagues, work space, and a secretary at least to answer the phone and take messages. How could you manage this? Reverse the logic we used for the consulting business and tell the department chair that you are developing a consulting business and want to continue your academic work at the same time. Do they have an office you could use part-time? Research space? You would be happy to do some administrative task for them, or be available to help some beleaguered colleague grade exams (think what you could barter and do it from the position of a colleague who is striking an equitable bargain). Since your gender is going to be used against you many times, I think it is ethical to use it in your favor when that is possible. If you have small children, your explanation could be that you want to continue your work while devoting more time to child care. If you have just moved to the area you may have followed your partner there and be looking for a regular position. In the meantime, could you be appointed to a nonsalaried research associate position so that you would have access to library facilities and letterhead for writing to research contacts? Your thesis supervisor and graduate faculty contacts can be helpful in contacting their friends and arranging for such a position for you as a favor. Make sure they tell the story you want associated with you in this position, because ideally you will use your contacts and this affiliation not just to keep yourself sane, but also as the springboard for other jobs just as you would have had you been employed by this institution.

Know what you need and go after it. Goal-directedness and a workable plan are invaluable in getting you that exciting job.

OUTSIDE ACADEME/INSIDE THE MAINSTREAM

There are many excellent reasons to be excited about the possibility of working in a corporate or industrial setting, not the least of which are the salary possibilities. A 1983 analysis of the demographic characteristics of the membership of a women's network organization in a moderate-sized Eastern city put the average (mean) age of the members at 40, the mean salary at $35,000 + , with a salary range of $11,000 to $148,000.

Why should you be excited by a corporate job?

Business is a different culture, and a different culture can be challenging and exciting, whether it is Sao Paolo or IBM.

Business offers the opportunity to change from a theoretical to an applied mode of operation, in which the work that you do has the possibility of effecting immediate change.

Business operates on a merit-based system. There is a high degree of accountability, and performance is rewarded.

Business rewards come in terms of status and money, and the power to make changes.

Your job responsibilities can change relatively frequently, so your work need not be boring. In the corporate world you don't have to look forward to teaching the same course for the next 10 years.

Your research and analytical skills are needed in the business world. Wouldn't it be nice to be paid for them?

The right business will offer you the opportunity to take risks, to try out new ideas, because the company knows it will benefit from your creativity.

The challenges and tasks of the corporate world can be as intellectually appealing as most you have worked on in your academic career, and possibly more so than many of them. You have not been educated simply in history or literature or sociology or French, you have been trained to think and question and solve dilemmas and juggle many pieces of data to find the critical common thread, the novel analysis, and you have been better trained at this than 95% of the population. It is the use of these skills which often is the most satisfying aspect of our work, with the material on which we exercise them secondary to the pleasure we derive. Analyzing why a group within your corporate structure has not been able to meet its quarterly plans for the last year, working on a solution which makes all the employees feel better about themselves and their work and which increases productivity by 27%, being able to follow through on you plan and see the results, and then getting an excellent performance review yourself with a concomitant merit raise can be as heady an experience as giving a well-taught course or completing a paper for publication, and it's not a significantly different experience (except for the feedback and the raise).

Business offers real support for your work in terms of resources. Instead of grease pencils on a transparency sheet, you can have access to a professional graphics department and an audiovisual division which will make your slide show into a video.

If you view business critically, joining the system offers the possibility of changing it to fit your ideal model. The female vice-president of a local moderate-sized company recently was able to order a review and analysis of her company's compensation system, and noted a significant difference between the salaries of occupations generally segregated by gender. Without ever using the red flag term of comparable worth, she was able to change the basis of that compensation system to reduce that wage differential substantially.

Many of us who grew up in the college days of the 1960s and 1970s learned to mistrust the corporate world. That blanket condemnation is as invalid as any other. The very best of human values make corporate sense. The most successful of businesses know that and, because of recent research reported in such books as Peters and Waterman's *In Search of Excellence* and Kanter's *The Change Masters*, the rest of the corporate world is learning it. You can be part of that.

To be part of that corporate world you have to understand it and how you might fit in. It is a formidable task, but you are good at learning. You have to learn what jobs exist in the corporate world, for which ones you have the skills, which you might want, and how to sell yourself into one of them.

Let's work backward. Business people understand why their work is interesting, but not why someone would leave an academic position with its prestige and perquisites. They also worry that a Ph.D.'s expectations will be too high for an entry-level position, which you will probably have to take to learn the ropes. A vice-president of a successful high-technology company suggested to me that he would be favorably impressed if someone with a humanities Ph.D., in an interview, or better still, in a cover letter, indicated a willingness to take an entry-level position, even if it meant a lateral or downward salary move. (With academic salaries as low as they are, however, it is unlikely that you would have to take a pay cut if you are at the junior faculty level.) Administration is different from management, and you must be able to communicate clearly and convincingly how this move fits into your career development plan.

Your task is to:

1. *Learn* more about the business world and what jobs exist there.
2. *Identify* your skills and develop a career plan.

3. *Develop* your curriculum vitae into a resume.

4. *Sell* yourself.

Remember — LIDS — that is what you are going to take off your possibilities. Let's look at each of these.

Learn

Where do you go to learn? Join the ASTD — its press offers excellent books and tapes — or join other professional associations in which you may be interested (see organizations listed in Appendixes). Too many? Too expensive? Go as someone's guest, or ask if you can attend meetings of specific interest to you. Definitely join your local professional women's network or Business and Professional Women's Association and talk to everyone about what work they do, what its requirements are, how they got there. People will think you a fascinating conversationalist. Get away from parties with only academicians and meet people in the corporate world and ask them what they do, what skills they use, what the job possibilities are. It is polite conversation.

Learn the vocabulary and language of this new environment. Its jargon is as exotic as that of your discipline, and as in academic situations, if you can't speak the language, you can't join the club. You'll need to be able to understand and to generate sentences like:

Our CEO went to our HRD manager with a request for a needs assessment. She thought that our matrix management structure suggested the need for team building before we initiated the quality circle plan.

Take a lesson from the anthropologists on learning the language of a new culture. Listen to their conversations and ask for clarifications, and read the writings. The books popular in 1985 were: Deal and Kennedy, *Corporate Cultures: The Rites and Rituals of Corporate Life*; Kanter, *Men and Women of the Corporation* and *The Change Masters*; Ouchi, *Theory Z*; Peters and Waterman, *In Search of Excellence*.

Read magazines such as *Working Woman* and *Savvy*, and industry and trade journals. Your reference librarian, or the librarian at local companies, can be of help in identifying these. This can be a boost to a whole new world. It *is* a different culture, and if you want to be accepted by the natives, you must not frighten them by your dress or conversation.

Both *Working Woman* and *Savvy* will give you good ideas on appropriate dress, and I think they are more realistic than *Dressing for Success*, which is overly rigid for most businesses. You need not be a clone, but neither can you be a sore thumb. I like to think of it as a matter of courtesy, rather like covering your head in St. Peter's.

Trade in your canvas bag for a briefcase, and buy a copy of Figler's *The Complete Job Search Handbook* and take it home in that briefcase. It will lead you into your next task.

Identify

Identify your skills and develop a career plan. Ideally this can be done with the help of a trained career counselor you find at a place like The Counseling Center of Hartford College for Women or your local YWCA or an independent consulting group. Be sure to ask the credentials and experience of any counselor before you make an appointment, and do not think you need a $1000 treatment. Services which charge very high fees are not noticeably better than those with reasonable fees.

In the absence of such professional help, or even to augment it, at The Counseling Center we recommend going through the exercises in Figler's *The Complete Job Search Handbook*. It offers clear, practical step-by-step tasks most people are willing to do, and as such is more useful than the more familiar, *What Color Is Your Parachute?* which is so formidable it is difficult to find anyone who has read it, much less followed all its suggestions. Figler will help you identify your skills and interests, will give you guidelines for matching these with jobs, and will guide you through a complete job search.

Again, activate your networks, the same ones I discussed under consulting. Tell everyone you are looking for a job, and what kind of a job. One woman who came to us mentioned her job search to her dentist, and she in turn mentioned it to another patient whose brother-in-law was looking for just such a person. The contact was made and she eventually got the job. A surprising number of jobs are filled via networks of acquaintances. Yours could be the next one.

There are many academic skills which translate to business. I have listed a number of these in Table 14.1. The items in parentheses are the academic translations.

TABLE 14.1   Some Academic Skills Which Translate to Business

Research
Problem solving (research)[a]
Inductive and deductive reasoning
Instructional planning (curriculum development)
Collaboration
Negotiation
Speaking
Writing clearly
Instructing
Teaching — breaking information into its components
   communication
   analysis and presentation of information
   motivating learners
   verbal skills (thinking on your feet)
   effective use of audiovisuals
   humor
Team leadership (committee work)
Coaching (supervising graduate students)
Performance evaluation
Editing
Budget control (responsible for grant or department budget of $ — —)
Policy planning
Conducting needs assessments
Perseverance
Intellectual capabilities

[a]Items in parentheses describe the academic activity.

The transition is possible:

Twyla Fletcher has a Ph.D. in economics and taught for eight years. She realized she didn't want to be in that environment for the rest of her life and investigated job possibilities in her area. She followed Figler's advice, made a career plan with both short- and long-term goals, changed her curriculum vitae to a resume, and took a relatively low-level job in the investments section of a regional bank. In two years she had learned enough about the business to be given a supervisory position, in three more years she was promoted to assistant vice-president in the same department. She recently accepted a lateral move as vice-president for personnel. Her economics training got her her first "real world" job, but is of little import in her current position, where her newly acquired management skills are most utilized. She is now earning twice the salary she commanded as an associate professor.

Develop

Develop your curriculum vitae into a resume, or better still, several resumes. You will in all likelihood be applying for several different jobs and the emphasis on each resume should be on the qualifications called for in that specific job. The best resource book for this task is Jackson's *The Perfect Resume*. Jackson will prepare you to write your resume, show you the different types (I think a functional resume is the most appropriate for an academician going into the business world), take you through the process, and show you how to write an effective cover letter which will enhance the possibility that someone will read the resume you have so carefully prepared. Read the book and follow his instructions. The ideal resume is one page long. I think that the resumes of academicians are often somewhat longer, but should not exceed two pages. A curriculum vitae and a resume contain very different information. Compare your vita format to the functional resume in Table 14.2. The names and locations have been changed. This resume tells the prospective employer what skills Jacqueline can bring to her job in communications, and does so clearly, positively, and concisely.

The language of resumes is very important. Table 14.3 contains a list of verbs, adjectives, and headings which can make your resume more impressive and positive. This is not the place for modesty.

Sell

Selling yourself into your next job will be your next step. You now have several cover letters and a revisable resume or several basic resumes for the various positions you will pursue. Now the task is to get the interview and sell yourself. Figler's *The Complete Job Search Handbook* will be of help again here as you prepare for your interviews. Investigating the company and practicing anwering the questions you are likely to be asked out loud to someone else are both essential. I don't care how well you are able to improvise in front of a class; in an interview it won't work. You must be prepared. Additional resources I have found helpful in interview preparation are Gray, Loeffler, and Cooper's *Every Woman Works*, a series of columns by Fader in *Working Woman* (August and October 1984), and an article by Lee, "Tough Questions and Hidden Tests Revealed," in *Ms.* magazine, June 1983.

TABLE 14.2 Sample of Curriculum Vitae Transformed into a Resume

Jacqueline Washington
472 Bailey Road
Arlington, Massachusetts 02174
(617)873-7372

CAREER OBJECTIVES:	Communication specialist in private sector using demonstrated skills in such areas as public relations, research and writing.
PUBLIC RELATIONS:	Developed advertising campaign, designed brochures, coordinated national media campaign and local media coverage for convention of 500 recruited from a large national professional organization. Designed brochures, wrote press releases and college newspaper copy for Elderhostel, a statewide summer college program for senior citizens with an enrollment of 850.
RESEARCH:	Conducted research on employment patterns of women reentering work force after child-bearing. Utilized major data bank and 50 current employees varying in age, race and socioeconomic status. Devised and conducted research for longitudinal study of these women over a five-year period, wrote and obtained a funding grant.
WRITING:	Published three articles in major scholarly journals. Wrote invited article for *Psychology Today*. Designed and wrote individualized 16-week study guide for large introductory course subsequently adopted by department. Edited sports section of *The Daily Sun*, Cornell University daily newspaper.[a]
PUBLIC SPEAKING:	Have presented invited talks on workplace dynamics, male and female employment patterns, African folklore, and Elderhostel to corporate seminars, professional associations, educational and civic groups.
PROGRAM MANAGEMENT:	Developed program with 14 invited national speakers and presented papers for a two-day major conference of professional organization. Coordinated a committee from a seven-state region, sucessfully delegated responsibility, maximized committee efficiency and facilitated decision making.[b]

(continued)

153

TABLE 14.2   (*Continued*)

Jacqueline Washington	Resume, p. 2

EMPLOYMENT:	1982–present. Assistant Professor, Psychology. Boston University, Boston, Massachusetts 1980–82. Assistant Professor, Psychology. Keuka College, Keuka Park, New York.
EDUCATION:	1980 Ph.D. from University of Michigan, Ann Arbor, Michigan Major field — Experimental Social Psychology Minor fields — Industrial Psychology Nonverbal communication 1977 M.Sc. from the University of Michigan Major field — Experimental Social Psychology Minor fields — Nonverbal communication Group process 1976 B.A. from Cornell University, Ithaca, New York Major field — Psychology
PUBLICATIONS:	(This section is optional. Papers should be listed individually only if they are directly relevant to the position for which you are applying. Jackie's are very academic and she will not include them).
PROFESSIONAL ORGANIZATIONS:	American Psychological Association, Association for Women in Psychology, Sigma Zi (scientific honorary society), American Association for the Advancement of Science.
REFERENCES:	Available on request.

[a]We are not listing an article Jackie wrote for the feminist newspaper *Off Our Backs*. You must make the decision about the inclusion of politically sensitive material in your resume, remembering that the resume serves a filtering function.
[b]What Jackie actually did was to chair the organizing committee for the national conference of the Association for Women in Psychology. Her program and program/paper review committee was from a seven-state region, and she organized them via conference calls and memos from her word processor so that they needed to have only two full-day meetings together to design and implement the national conference. Her task here was to present this accomplishment in the most professional skill-oriented manner, and it translates to the Program Management paragraph in her resume.

TABLE 14.3 Critical Words for Resumes

ACTION WORDS

actively	eliminate	motivate	responsible
accelerate	establish	organize	responsibilities
adapt	evaluate	originate	revise
administer	expand	participate	review
analyze	expedite	perform	schedule
approve	found	plan	significantly
coordinate	generate	pinpoint	simplicity
conceive	increase	program	set up
conduct	influence	propose	solve
complete	implement	prove	strategy
control	interpret	provide	structure
create	improve	proficient	streamline
delegate	launch	recommend	successfully
develop	lead	reduce	supervise
demonstrate	lecture	reinforce	support
direct	maintain	reorganize	teach
effect	manage	revamp	

SELF-DESCRIPTIVE WORDS

active	determined	independent	realistic
adaptable	diplomatic	logical	reliable
aggressive	disciplined	loyal	resourceful
alert	discrete	mature	respective
ambitious	economical	methodical	self-reliant
analytical	efficient	objective	sense of humor
attentive	energetic	optimistic	sincere
broad-minded	enterprising	perceptive	sophisticated
conscientious	enthusiastic	personable	systematic
consistent	extroverted	pleasant	tactful
constructive	fair	positive	talented
creative	forceful	practical	will travel
dependable	imaginative	productive	will relocate

SAMPLE LIST OF FUNCTIONAL HEADINGS

Management	Supervision	Promotion
Advertising	Organization	Investment
Administrative	Purchasing	Graphic design
Public relations	Acquisition	Printing
Accounting	Planning	Layout
Communication	Scheduling	Market research
Engineering	Employment	Instruction
Writing and editing	Public speaking	Programming
Research	Fund raising	Presentations

(continued)

TABLE 14.3 (*Continued*)

Finance	Community affairs	Architecture
Counseling	Teaching	Program development
Electronics	Systems and procedures	Chemistry
Data processing	Product development	Social work
Publicity		

Compiled by The Counseling Center, Hartford College for Women, 1985.

GETTING THROUGH

Remember to reward yourself. Looking for a job is a full-time job itself, and it is fraught with potential disappointments and blows to the ego. It is exhausting. Exercise. Nurture yourself through it. Give yourself tasks and reward yourself for tasks completed. These principles work in our lives as well as in psychology laboratories.

The resources out there to help you make this transition to a different mainstream are abundant. The road is rocky but entirely passable, especially with a good plan and the help of friends. And the view from the new hilltop is expansive and exciting. Go for it!

REFERENCES AND ADDITIONAL RESOURCES

Bestor, D. (1982). *Aside from teaching, what in the world can you do?* Seattle, WA: University of Washington Press. (Career strategies for liberal arts graduates.)

Blake, R. R., & Mouton, J. S. (1983). *Consultation* (2nd ed.). Reading, MA: Addison-Wesley.

Bolles, R. N. (1984). *What color is your parachute? A practical manual for job hunters and career changers.* Berkeley, CA: Ten Speed Press.

Burg, D. (1983, Dec.). When the ax falls. . . . *Working Woman*, pp. 100–104.

Business Directories
  College Placement Annual
  Dun & Bradstreet Directories
  Fortune's Plant and Product Directory
  MacRae's Blue Book
  Standard & Poor's Directories
  Thomas' Register of American Manufacturers

Deal, T. E., & Kennedy, A. A. (1982). *Corporate cultures: The rites and rituals of corporate life.* Reading, MA: Addison-Wesley.

Dictionary of occupational titles. Washington, DC: Superintendent of Public Documents. (Contains alphabetically organized list of over 20,000 occupations, with job descriptions and training requirements. Read the instructions first.)

Fader, S. S. (1984, Aug.). Start here: The big interview. *Working Woman*, pp. 49–50.

Fader, S. S. (1984, Oct.). Start here: Fielding tough questions. *Working Woman*, pp. 64–67.

Figler, H. (1981). *The complete job search handbook.* New York: Holt, Rinehart & Winston.

Gallessich, J. (1982). *The profession and practice of consultation.* San Francisco: Jossey-Bass.

Gray, B, Loeffler, D., & Cooper, R. (1982). *Every woman works.* Belmont, CA: Lifetime Learning Publications.

Harragan, B. (1977). *Games mother never taught you.* New York: Warner Books.

Irish, R. K. (1973). *Go hire yourself an employer.* Garden City, NY: Anchor Books.

Jackson, T. (1981). *The perfect resume.* Garden City, NY: Anchor Books.

Kanter, R. M. (1977). *Men and women of the corporation.* New York: Basic Books. (Now a classic introduction to the corporate setting.)

Kanter, R. M. (1983). *The change masters: Innovations for productivity in the American corporation.* New York: Simon & Schuster.

Lathrop, R. (1977). *Who's hiring who?* Berkeley, CA: Ten Speed Press.

Lee, M. (1983, June). Tough questions and hidden tests revealed. *Ms.*, pp. 50–72.

Molloy, J. T. (1978). *Women's dress for success.* New York: Warner Books.

Ouchi, W. G. (1982). *Theory Z.* New York: Avon. (The Japanese management challenge to American business.)

Peters, T. J., & Waterman, R. H. (1982). *In search of excellence: Lessons from America's best-run companies.* New York: Harper & Row.

Silcox, D. (1980). *Woman time: Personal time management for women only.* Ridgefield, NJ: Wyden.

U.S. Department of Labor. *The occupational outlook handbook.* Washington, DC.: Author. (Published biannually, this publication contains information on the nature of the work, national job trends, training requirements, earnings, and places to write for further information for hundreds of jobs.)

U.S. Department of Labor. *The occupational outlook quarterly.* Washington, DC.: Author. (Contains even more information, especially on new jobs.)

Winston, S. (1979). *The entrepreneurial woman.* New York: Newsweek Books.

■ 15
Relocations: Professional, Geographic, Personal

SUSAN GORE

I have been responding creatively to the challenge of academic job scarcity since mailing out the first of the 500 or so applications I submitted as I completed my Ph.D. in social psychology in 1975. Although I did find an academic job, I still have the resulting batch of form rejection letters. Someday I swear I will wallpaper a bathroom with them.

My life as a full-time academic ended in 1981. Since then, I have written at least that many applications again. In the past three years I have been director of a nonprofit association, a convention coordinator for the American Association of University Women, a computer consultant, a fundraiser, an Organizational Development consultant, a relocation seminar creator, and a member of the ranks of the unemployed. During that same three-year period, I have lived in Italy, West Germany, Washington, D.C., Crowley, Texas, and Oakland, California.

To some, such continual change may create an image of perpetual crisis. I prefer to describe my life as never dull. In any case, in Chinese the word "crisis" is formed by combining two characters signifying "danger" and "opportunity." If there is anything I have learned through my experiences, it is that any significant change or life event carries both of these elements. What I would like to share are some of the strategies I have evolved for utilizing both the danger and the opportunities encountered in my continuing search for the perfect job.

Generalizations about how to find meaningful work and/or relocate successfully are difficult to make. Definitions of 'success" are as diverse as the individuals experiencing it. In addition, the experience of relocating is influenced by both personal and situational factors. Personality variables like self-confidence, willingness to accept help, tolerance for ambiguity and change, sociability, and flexibility typically reduce the stress of starting over.

Another factor affecting the change is whether you are newly initiated into the ranks of the Ph.D. or are someone with 5 to 10 years of experience. If you are a new Ph.D., you might have more youth and energy, and a greater willingness to explore different options than someone who has invested years creating a professional reputation and personal niche as a scholar. On the other hand, if you have 5 to 10 years of experience, you have the advantage of being able to present potential employers with a track record of accomplishments. Of course, the trick is how to relate what you have been doing to where you want to go next — once you've figured that out.

Lastly, believing that you have a choice about professional or geographic relocations plays a major role in how you will feel. Even in the face of academic cutbacks, you can exercise choice in terms of what alternatives you consider.

PRIVILEGE AND DISCIPLINE

If you are contemplating leaving academe, it is important that you weigh the benefits and costs carefully. My experiences within and outside academe have made me more cognizant of the truly privileged environment campus life affords. The privilege is not in terms of money or immediately visibile influence — it is in having control over how you spend your time. The concept of a compulsory 8-to-5 workday five days a week is still foreign to most universities, as is top-down assignment of the content of your work. If you want to teach a course on American women authors 1900–1980, you may have to jump a number of curriculum committee hoops. However, if you want to make those authors the focus of your existing course on 20th-century American authors, the time-honored traditions of academic freedom and tenure practically guarantee your ability to do so. The majority of American workers don't have these privileges, even at the professional level. On the positive side, working a regular work week may produce a pleasant surprise — nights and weekends previously devoted to work can be reclaimed. And the financial rewards outside academe can be considerable.

When deciding whether or not to leave academe, take into account the following questions: How important is it to you to have control over how you spend your work time and what you spend it doing? How important are the trade-offs? How can you find or create a situation that provides a combination that works best for you?

One exercise that was helpful to me in determining what career direction to take consisted of writing my own obituary, as I would like to have it read (Irish, 1978). The result was both surprising and portentous. I identified two life goals in the 1980 obituary I wrote: to be director of the National Women's Studies Association and to be on the Board of *Ms.* magazine. I since have accomplished one of those goals. The priorities and experiences I hope to have in my life also were clarified. The importance and shape of family were revealed in my list of survivors. This particular exercise was important because it set an outer boundary around my life, a hypothetical time frame within which all I might want to happen must occur.

If you decide your goals can be met by a nonacademic career, the resources you need are at hand. The discipline you have learned from academic work will be your most valuable asset. Moving out of academe is 90% perspiration and 10% inspiration, as my 10th-grade English teacher admonished. The basic academic skills of collecting large amounts of new information and assimilating it can be applied directly to the task of developing a new career.

CAREER RELOCATIONS

Job searches come in two shapes, both overwhelmingly big. The mass mailing approach is one of these; highly targeted, intense personal networking is the other.

Mass Mailings

A mass mailing is what I did as I finished graduate school, applying to essentially all vacancies for an academic social psychologist. The main assumptions underlying this approach are that all jobs are basically alike and that the law of averages ensures some successes in a large enough number of attempts. In fact, the law of averages works. The result may be a more eclectic collection of alternatives than a highly targeted approach, but more interesting surprises are likely to turn up in a far-flung net than from casting a single line. If you do not know exactly what you want to do outside academe or all the ways to translate your skills into nonacademic expertise, a mass mailing job search has a lot to recommend it.

As the name implies, the logistics of this approach are massive. First, even a scattergun has to be pointed in some direction. The accomplishments, skills, and priorities reflected in your obituary will provide useful guidance here. Now it's time to collect information on the universe of potential employers you have identified—company statistics, employment policies, and procedures.

Just as when applying for college or graduate school, there are numerous reference sources to aid your search. Annual reports provide a wealth of basic information. Most cities have a business library or business sections in the general library crammed with volumes like *The Index of Occupational Titles* (there are over 20,000), *Contacts Influential*, and A. M. Best's *Agents Guide to Life Insurance Companies*. Useful business magazines include *Harvard Business Review*, *Forbes* (especially the annual business ratings issue), *Fortune*, *Business Week*, *Inc.* magazine, and *Mother Jones*. Each set of professions has its own set of journals or trade publications, too. Less exotic but often useful are the Yellow Pages.

For those interested in the nonprofit world outside academe, general libraries carry resources similar to those described for business. New York and San Francisco also have Foundation Center offices containing annual reports and additional information on hundreds of public and private philanthropic institutions. Some of these same resources may be available at your university from the research office.

While I don't generally recommend the use of "executive search" services, in some circumstances they can be an effective career-change strategy. Two situations that may make executive search assistance worthwhile are being too traumatized to accomplish the tasks I have described or having extremely tight time or financial constraints. However, no matter what representatives of executive search firms may tell you about personal attention, they operate much like institutionalized mass mailing approaches. You will be one of a large number of clients being presented to an equally large number of potential employers. One of the first questions an agency manager will ask you is "Can you be counted on to accept any offer obtained for you by the firm?" They will be looking for an affirmative answer, which gives you little control over the search. Firms that charge you a fee without regard to the outcome of their services put less pressure on you than employer-paid services. The difference is relatively small, however; large numbers of clients and fast turnover is characteristic of the executive search game. Knowing this when you go is important to your ability to evaluate what these firms will and won't do, and whether you can utilize what they offer.

A mass mailing approach is relatively impersonal whether you or a search firm handles it. Critical to your success, then, is having an attention-grabbing cover letter and resume. If necessary, get a professional service to write your resume for you. However, I strongly recommend that you write your own resume. If you feel inadequate in the face of this task, scan several of the many books available on the topic or talk with people in the field of interest to you and ask for a sample of a good resume.

Having an answering machine is another indispensable job-search tool. Avoid cute or highly personal outgoing messages. You should project the same crisp dynamism on your answering machine message as in your cover letters and resumes. Return calls promptly in a businesslike manner. That means, first, assume whoever called you did so because they are interested (that builds self-confidence) and, second, do not assume any particular call is the answer to your prayers. Desperation or overconfidence comes through the telephone. You are engaging in a complicated dance. The steps are ritualized, designed to provide information about the next step.

A Targeted Search

The primary alternative to a mass assault on the job market is a highly targeted personal approach. You don't have to be a world-class networker to get results from the personal approach; much of the secret to success is simply dogged persistence. In the personal approach everything you ever learned about polite behavior such as punctuality, attentive listening, and thank-you notes takes on heightened importance.

The main assumption underlying a targeted approach to career change is that you have a clearly identified target of *some* sort. For instance, you must know what kind(s) of work you want to do, for whom you want to work, how much money you want to make, or where you want to live.

Corollary assumptions are that impressing a few key people favorably is at least as effective as turning out massive numbers of impersonal letters, that the truly interesting jobs in this world are rarely posted publicly, and that even if posted, in most cases they are likely to go to the person with inside connections.

It would be erroneous to infer from this that ability is irrelevant in a targeted search. Rather, the assumption is that the candidates with whom you are competing for any given position *all* possess excellent credentials. Thus, anyone without something extra is virtually indistinguishable from the herd.

Reviewing your own skills with a fresh eye is one way to use what is unique about your experience to your benefit. For example, suppose you are an English Ph.D. with an interest in publishing. You are moderately well-published in academic journals (six articles in five years). You have reviewed the same number of articles, one for a journal edited by a colleague whose work you admire and with whom you have become friendly. You write poetry for private pleasure at home on your word processor. You are proud of the last accomplishment, because you remember how garbled the user's manual was at instructing you how to make the computer work. In fact, you ultimately created a one-page outline of the program for yourself to make the manual usable.

What extras do you see even in this limited amount of information that could be used in a targeted search? Two seem apparent. Having developed a personal as well as professional relationship with an editor may be your ticket out of academe. First, your friend is likely to write a glowing reference and to produce as many individually addressed copies as you need.(A "Dear Colleague" version also would make an excellent addition to your mass mailing packet.) She or he also will know publishers who may have openings or who at least will meet with you for an "informational interview" (described below). Those people know other people . . . and your network grows.

If our hypothetical English professor is interested in technical writing, a second gambit she might try is to include in her resume something like "Wrote technical guide for Lotus 1–2–3" or whatever program she translated from user's manual jargon. If she is really bold she would mention it in her cover letter, too. Is this stretching the truth? Perhaps, but did the "real" user's manual author, in fact, write a usable manual? Some publisher obviously thought so, and might think the same of her — or your — work.

The goal of this resume-writing tactic is to relate your academic skills to the "real world" tasks of your target employers through a specific examples. (See Shepela's chapter for further suggestions.) What if your tactic works so well an employer asks to see your user's guide? I would put it into some semblance of manual format if it isn't already, print a clean copy, and present it proudly, preferably in person. Use it as a reason for a second interview! Be prepared on paper or in person to point out how and why your version is better from the perspective of the average consumer — you.

Critical tasks in using the targeted approach successfully are identifying the relevant key people and conveying your abilities and goals to them effectively. You should also learn as much as possible about each prospective employer or company. Requesting an informational interview is very useful here. The stated purpose of such interviews is *not* to be hired for an existing vacancy, but primarily to enable you to learn about a company or field.

I rate informational interviews as highly as love and electricity in terms of helping to survive a career change. At least in theory, you are not being sized up for a job. The amount of pressure this takes off both you and the person you are seeing is tremendous. How better to learn the jargon of an entirely new field under nonthreatening conditions? Where better to ask questions you "can't" ask in a real job interview: "What drives people crazy about being a ____?" "How do you think my background and personality would fit into being a ____ or working for ____?" "How do you think my resume could be improved?" "Whom do you know that I should talk to next? (in general or at a specific company)" Be bold. Allow yourself to enjoy learning everything you can about this new field that just might become your next life's work.

At the same time, always present yourself as a professional. Good managers are always looking for valuable new additions to their staff. There may be a vacancy you don't know about. Positions have been created more than once for the right person. Or your informational contact might result in a referral leading to the job of your dreams. So enjoy — and cherish — the informational interview.

Where does the wondrous process of target interviewing begin? Past personal contacts are the best place to start. One guideline I use in evaluating previously unknown contacts is to make sure I follow up on those I hear about from three different sources. Another is to trust my instincts in individual interactions. Personal chemistry, serendipity, and persistence also have major roles to play in any job search.

Telephone and personal contacts, not the written word, are primary in a targeted job search. On a daily basis, I have discovered a pattern as to how my time is spent. The morning, until approximately 11 a.m., is for making telephone calls to initiate or follow up on inquiries about job openings and to contact individuals to whom I have been referred. Midday through the afternoon is spent in appointments. I prefer to combine lunch or coffee breaks with these meetings because eating or drinking injects informality. I always go planning to pay (keeping good records for income tax purposes), but acquiese if my partner prefers to split the bill or handle it her/himself. If someone prefers an office appointment, I keep it to half an hour unless they indicate otherwise and put extra effort into coming with as well-developed questions as possible. In both cases, thank-you notes go out immediately afterward.

Continuing contacts are an important part of targeted searches. Sending newspaper clippings or other notices of mutual interest is appropriate, as is calling if you have information beneficial to their work. In interviewing for currently available positions, keeping in close contact is even more helpful for demonstrating your genuine interest and initiative.

While fewer items go into the mail in targeted searches compared to mass ones, composing resumes and cover letters is akin to an art form in a targeted search. Each resume may need to be tailored to the position available, not simply the cover letter. Again, make sure both represent yourself vividly in relation to the position *and* the employer's particular needs.

As you can see, a targeted search is not quicker or simpler than a mass mailing approach. Both are full-time jobs. Thinking about your career change as a temporary full-time job actually is a useful strategy to avoid becoming bogged down in the morass of seemingly endless details and the inevitable disappointments you will experience. You have survived both before and will again.

GEOGRAPHIC RELOCATIONS

The mere mention of moving generally elicits reactions ranging from groans to adamant refusal. The thought of packing up objects accumulated over time is exhausting, heightened midway through the process by the discovery that one's possessions have multiplied beyond comprehension, like coathangers breeding behind closet doors. If the move is motivated by external forces, disrupting long-established career and living patterns, the psychological, emotional, and relationship aspects take on even greater importance than the physical. You can, at least, pay someone to handle the physical work. Ultimately, only you can experience and make sense of the rest.

I know of individuals who have spent two years laying the groundwork for a move and couldn't imagine doing it another way. One such woman, Judy, was teaching history at a North Carolina university. She decided she wanted to move into training and to the West Coast. Judy began by joining the American Society for Training and Development (ASTD), the field's main professional association, and volunteering for committees responsible for organizing local training conferences. Her volunteer training evolved into paid consulting done generally on weekends, in addition to her full-time academic work. A year's worth of reading of corporate annual reports and free practice training later, Judy decided her goals closely matched those of the Levi Strauss & Company, headquartered in San Francisco.

Judy contacted Levi Strauss's personnel department by mail to obtain application materials and then by telephone to learn who was in charge of training. A letter to the manager of training followed, asking for an informational interview while she would be visiting San Francisco during a specified week. A follow-up call confirmed the interview day and time as well as giving Judy a preliminary feeling for the person she would meet. Several questions she had distilled from reading about Levi Strauss also got answered during the call, including whether she would be able to observe any training sessions or meet other members of the department.

The informational interview went well. Judy learned that there were no positions currently available, but that a reorganization was anticipated within the year. Judy returned to North Carolina and immediately sent thank-you notes to everyone she had met at Levi's. A longer letter went to the Training Manager, expressing Judy's appreciation, her interest in Levi Strauss, and her intention to stay in close contact regarding the reorganization. A year later, after three more trips to the West Coast, Judy was offered a job in the training department of Levi Strauss and Company. When asked if it was worth the time and expense, her response is an unequivocal, "No question about it!"

This story is unusual in its simplicity, but not unique. Focused personal desire can be an awesome force. It is no guarantee of success, nor is it the only path, however. There is truth in popular wisdom about the importance of being visible, available, and able to take advantage of unanticipated openings or contacts by first locating where you want to be.

As basic as it may seem, do not forget to provide as many supports for yourself as possible when making major geographic, as well as career, changes. For example, my most recent move occurred as a result of a personal relationship; I moved without a job, trusting my past history of success to hold true. An important support I gave myself in the process was to project a six-month job search. With that projection I gave myself not only a realistic time frame but permission not to take offers I didn't want and to keep looking without feeling I'd failed if the perfect job didn't appear immediately.

Deciding on a six-month term was a subjective process, aided by advice from friends, books, and professionals in career placement. The "best" length for any individual depends on factors like where the search is taking place, the state of that job market and overall economy, the level of position sought (entry, management, executive), income requirements, and whether the search is "cold" or assisted in various ways. Time frames must be flexible, too. A six month plan does not imply turning down good offers "because it's not time yet," nor panicking into acceptance of any offer "because it is time." In fact, I have discovered I use several time frames in evaluation of my job-search progress, including a set of five-year goals for my life. In that regard, I don't expect the "time frame" of my search for the work I want to do in my life ever to have an end.

RELATIONSHIPS

It is hard to evaluate how sharing personal and professional transitions with a partner will affect either the relationship or the decisions made. In some ways, having a partner increases the complexity of such decisions geometrically; in others, having the personal and/or economic support of another individual or group may be what makes a career or geographic change possible. My own experience has been mixed.

In 1975, I was married and finishing my Ph.D. In August I got what I considered a good offer to teach at a university about four hours away from where we currently lived. My husband and I had talked earlier in my graduate career about the dual-career dilemma of who moves for whom. As an electrical engineer, he felt he was far more mobile career-wise than I, and I agreed. As I began sending out vitae, however, Ron got nervous. A Southerner, like myself, he really wasn't sure he could live in New York City. Or Boston. Or Dallas. Or Los Angeles.

As my job search continued, the list of places Ron couldn't consider became longer. What confused me further was Ron's frequently stated loathing for his current job and disaffection with Nashville. My career/geographic decision also became a marital choice. In the process, both Ron and I came to the realization that while he had thought he would leave his job and relocate based on my career, it was not something he actually was willing to do.

The moral of this story, in my opinion, is that the effects of career and geographic change can be insidious. Conflicts cropping up in relationships often may relate less to the apparent problem than to the exploration of previously untested values and priorities, as well as to the intense pressures created by uncertainty and change. Situationally, there are the stresses of moving and adjusting to an unfamiliar place where your entire map of where things are and personal and professional networks have to be recreated. No wonder some people hate to move!

Is there a solution? My bias favors talking things out as fully as possible, even seeking professional help if necessary. Identifying the complex personal and situational stresses created by relocation or career change and negotiating what to do about them is not easy, especially when the crunch is on to reach and implement a decision. Nowhere is the duality of "crisis" as representing both danger and opportunity more apparent.

CONCLUSIONS

Some women can transcend the difficult passages of career changes, never seeming to miss a beat. For most, however, it is not an easy time. Here, the discipline you exercised in graduate school is a quality to be appreciated. More than anything else, success requires keeping at whatever it is you are trying to do, be it a career transition, maintaining a significant relationship, or even figuring out what it is you are trying to do. Working smart or working hard, it is genuinely work. Capitalize on the many capabilities you have developed in becoming an academic. Those abilities, plus persistence, luck, and a little help at propitious times, are the most important ingredients for ensuring that your rewards are commensurate with not only your efforts but your dreams.

REFERENCE

Irish, R. (1978). *Go hire yourself an employer*. New York: Doubleday.

■ 16
Career Options and Strategies in Business and Management

LAURIE LARWOOD

Many academic scholars have long believed that working for a private business organization is a fearful experience. First, taking such a job has been equated with selling out humanitarian ideals in favor of advancing the power of monolithic Corporate Enterprise. The tasks put to us in business are repetitive, mind-numbing experiences from which few ever return. If the worst were to befall, and one had to look for such a job, the organization probably wouldn't want anyone with a degree such as ours anyway.

Like other myths, the mental barriers set up between scholars and management have some truth. Jobs in which the profit motive is paramount may unsettle those viewing human welfare or service as critical. Some of the work may be intellectually barren or, worse, counter to our values. For their part, organizations are sometimes at a loss as to how to productively employ Ph.D. specialists. On the other hand, where is it written that scholars must take vows of poverty? — that human welfare is unprofitable? — or that those who elect to remain in university life can also choose to ignore measures of efficiency and success? While some organizations may operate counter to our values, others do not; those who favor military research as well as those who oppose it can find business organizations to suit themselves. Well-run organizations recognize that work can be mind-numbing and try to optimize (or even to stretch) the fit between their human resources and the tasks challenging them.

The fact is, business functions by organizing resources — including people and their efforts and creative ideas — in the service of a goal such as building an automobile or operating a hospital. In a competitive economy, if the goal is accomplished sufficiently well, the business will attract more customers and be more profitable, enabling it to survive and grow. Growth in turn rewards those whose efforts succeeded. Unless it is very fortunate, a "dumb" business cannot grow very far. Instead, the business needs to seek out those who are bright, have the ideas, and are willing to commit themselves to it. It must keep the enthusiasm of these people and cannot afford to apply them to worthless or uninteresting tasks for long.

But are business and management consistent with a Ph.D.? In a word: absolutely. The degree itself is welcome but unnecessary; the knowledge, attitudes and creativity for which the degree stands are essential. The management function of business (managing people) is an almost perfect fit with the social sciences — especially psychology, sociology, political science, and economics.[1] In order to manage smoothly, one must be able to understand and work with subordinates, peers, and employers. The motivations, status structures, intrigues, and decision structures prominently studied in social science disciplines can all be brought to bear on problems.

General or overall line management can apply to many different disciplines precisely because it is not specialized. In smaller organizations, there may be opportunity for specialization, but in organizations employing more than a few hundred people, there is room to actually practice the specialty in which one is trained. For example, advertising, marketing, and public relations are becoming very receptive to those with degrees in literature and composition, psychology, film, and statistics. Ph.D. social workers, nurses, and psychologists are employed by most larger organizations as counselors; sociologists and psychologists are increasingly involved in the personnel departments of established firms in problems involving career development. A growing number of firms are seeking

[1]The present chapter considers those with degrees other than in the sciences, mathematics, medicine, engineering, or business. Individuals with the excluded degrees historically have found a welcome in industry and apparently understand very well how to blend academic and business interests.

professionals to set up day care, nutrition, and physical training programs for their employees and their families. Political science professionals find themselves welcome in strategic planning departments; historians are often engaged in recording and researching the organization's roots.

You don't have to graduate from a business school in order to find a worthwhile position in industry. What you do need is to investigate how the organization can apply someone with your combination of talents. Then you have to convince the persons making the hiring decision that they need you. The two phases are not necessarily accomplished simultaneously.

WHERE SCHOLARS ARE HIRED IN INDUSTRY

There are an unlimited number of potential positions open for the person able to convince someone that she can do the job. Moreover, many people take positions that do not precisely fit their skills when they are assured of being able to work their way into a better position later. If an actor can become President, a scholar should also be able to handle many positions. Nonetheless, some of the best entry-level person/job fits are often obtained in the following areas.

Advertising

Most large advertising and some public relations firms employ Ph.D.s and master's level people in a variety of positions. Basic advertising research involves applying the techniques of cognitive psychologists to measure responses to actual or potential advertising. Similar research is undertaken by agencies (or by related consulting firms used by the smaller agencies) to determine optimal product packaging, in-store placement, and recall of competitive messages. Advertising and public relations (together increasingly referred to as "marketing communications") rely on the finest writers they can find and are not shy about using Ph.D.s in literature and proven fiction writers.

Marketing

Marketing is a close kin of advertising — some manufacturing and retailing firms have their own in-house advertising staffs, while most handle marketing internally and coordinate with outside advertising agencies.

Marketing involves determining customer preferences and needs, and ensuring that the organization meets those needs. Important positions for psychologists, sociologists, and demographers include consumer behavior research (what are the demographics for this product or service, and how does the consumer react to it?), competitive research (surveying where your product or service stands in the marketplace and in the consumer's mind relative to alternatives), and the design of products, services, advertisements, and promotions to appeal to the apparent needs of the consumer. Both marketing and advertising use statisticians, programmers, and librarians to set up and maintain research, data bases, and resource libraries.

Human Factors

It is widely held that human-factors research (determining the limitations of human ability and physique) disappeared with the advent of radar and the end of the need to be certain that human volunteers don't fall asleep while visually tracking enemy aircraft. As usual, the reports were premature. Most large manufacturing firms (and many private consulting organizations) are heavily involved in human-factors work. Aerospace firms, for example, employ psychologists to ensure that pilots have the view needed from their cockpits of both the outside and instruments. Human-factors specialists have designed the seats with a view to comfort, cost, and weight. The interior decor has been designed to seem spacious. The instructions on the emergency cards have been carefully tested to ensure that they can be quickly understood by someone who cannot read. Physiologists and environmental health specialists are also employed on these projects. The most common uses of human-factors research are found in large-volume manufacturers (such as those making theater chairs) and in manufacturers of critical or lifesaving devices (such as manufacturers of medical and military equipment).

Human Resource Management

The old personnel area is giving way to a new concept. Rather than merely administer face-valid surveys and keep track of payroll deductions, HRM is now in charge of the human side of the business in over half of major corporations. These organizations are keenly aware of the need to take a holistic view to the utilization of people, and they seek researchers and specialists who can apply state-of-the-art techniques. Those with

Ph.D.s or related degrees in industrial/organizational, social, personality, and counseling psychology, social work, and education have the edge over those with other specialties. The aspects of HRM which are most frequently encountered include career development (through what path should people be promoted to ensure that they are fully trained when they reach the top?), testing (how can we develop valid tests or best use evaluation centers?), affirmative action (what does it take to be certain that hiring and promotion are blind to sex and race — or to encourage under-represented groups?), training (what are the best techniques for being certain that people understand what to do?), and motivation (how can we design compensation programs that are motivating to both new recruits and those nearing retirement?). As with other activities, smaller organizations are less frequently able to use specialists within their specialty, but allow them to apply their perspective across more general questions. At the moment smaller firms are also in touch with the HRM revolution, making it one of the three or four most important central activities of the organization — in terms of the field, converting it from a sleepy staff backwater to an important line operation.

Organizational Behavior and Organization Development

Unless you've had some experience, you probably won't be ready for this one, but a number of firms have personnel engaged in internal management consulting. The concept is to provide that person (often through the HRM Department) with free rein to examine the human systems and interactions throughout the organization. The internal consultant can either suggest necessary changes prescriptively (organizational behavior), or suggest and apply the processes needed to effect a change which need not be based on a prior prescription of what is needed (organizational development). Internal consultants also work on problem-oriented projects such as evaluating communications patterns within and between departments, and implementing more efficient structures to address the needs uncovered. The work involves diagnosis, information gathering, analysis, and program-development skills and can include activities such as building work teams, restructuring work methods, and developing problem-solving skills. A wide range of academic backgrounds are useful entry points: hands-on experience in the techniques and a degree in political science, industrial/organizational, social, or clinical psychology, sociology, or communications are usually preferred. Private management consulting firms and the larger accounting firms also have individuals engaged in these activities for clients. People lacking the ideal academic training have frequently gained entry to this area by working with individual private consultants as an assistant on a job-to-job basis (not for free — the fees are astounding).

Other Possibilities

If the discussion above did not meet your interest, the alternatives are limited only by your imagination. Begin with the recognition that anyone with research skills can find a place to use them. While this discussion has centered primarily on social science, don't let that fool you. Research skill in history and/or library science can pay off handsomely — nearly 100% of the largest 1,000 firms have active corporate libraries, many of which are larger and better funded than all but a handful of public and university libraries. If your interest is in social welfare, you are fortunate that most organizations employ people to take charge of corporate philanthropy. Increasingly, organizations are employing ethicists to try to balance the realities of business competition against what they see as the uncertainties of what should be done. Criminal justice researchers will find a welcome among organizations concerned that their lax controls may have allowed theft from the organization — or by the organization.

As a rule, those with Ph.D.s always have two possibilities open to them. They can choose to apply the techniques which are intrinsic to their discipline. For example, a literature Ph.D. has developed unusual writing skills, a psychologist has critical skills in devising and analyzing behavioral research, while an artist has developed an esthetic sense concerning color and form. Any task within an organization which can benefit from these abilities provides potential entree into the firm for the academic willing to move to industry. Because academic salaries are low, almost any skill will be worth at least as much to a firm as it is to a university at the Assistant Professor rank. With a few years experience, you should be able to command at least twice that amount.

The second possibility is to ply your specific research interests within the firm. Here the opportunities are more limited, and you will need to hunt for particular firms or classes of firms which need your specialized expertise. On the other hand, if you are in love with your research and are concerned with having to leave it for the sake of earning a living, this gives you the chance to have your cake and eat it, too. Some obvious examples follow, but you can (and should) make up your own to suit your interests: a psychologist researching sports medicine could work for several sporting goods manufacturers, larger hospitals, medical supply houses, and the three American automobile manufacturers; an historian specializing in the Far East can work with a number of trading firms currently focusing on China and interested in avoiding offense to delicate relationships; a sociologist researching inner-city problems can work with large contractors, urban renewal architects, and city planning agencies — and some large local employers; philosophers and others studying the relationships between criminal behavior and motivation can do it for any large retailer (and many other large employers), some insurors, or several manufacturers of security devices. Recognizing the former academic's need to stay current and to sometimes deviate in the direction of esoterica, the more enlightened employers frequently provide Ph.D.s with extra time for private research and often support academic conference participation.

CONVINCING THEM TO HIRE YOU

There is a key concept that separates many excellent people from an equally top job. They believe that if they are good at what they do, the world should believe them to be good and reward them, thus placing the emphasis on "good." What they must learn to do is place the emphasis on "believe" — if they are believed to be good, they are good and should be rewarded for it. In other words, credibility leads to success.

People making hiring decisions in management have an array of candidates from which to choose and limited information and time with which to make their decisions. First appearances, familiarity, and prior activities weigh heavily in the decisional process. The strong incentive to avoid an obvious mistake is also an incentive against experimentation. Finally, many management tasks cannot be readily evaluated as to success or failure; even if the task were judged, it may be difficult to place responsibility. Thus, decision makers are likely to prefer people who "look like they can do the job" — preferably with business degrees and business experience, who have no obvious strikes against them, and who have in the past been associated with increasingly important and successful projects (or who have decamped before the project failed). Despite an effort to appear objective, personnel decisions at the management level are largely subjective.

Here are your tools for cutting through this subjectivity.

Resume

Unless you are asked for a vita or know that the decision maker is a recent Ph.D., you are usually safer to use a resume than a vita. The latter stamps you as another wooly-headed academic lost in the management jungle, while the resume says that you are ready to abandon all of that. The resume should be accomplishment-oriented and brief (one page if possible); because appearances are important, be certain that it looks impressive at a glance and consider professional typesetting.

References

Don't provide references until they are asked for. Highly ranked people in the firm or well-known people in the industry are the most impressive references. After that, go for high titles in the university (Deans beat department heads). Be certain that your referee will say nothing negative about you (but be sure that the employer does not find out if you have obtained a copy of the reference as this will diminish its credibility; Shaffer & Tomarelli, 1981). Even your best friend may not know that a recommendation with anything negative is likely to cut your success rate substantially (Bolster & Springbett, 1961). Fortunately, a large proportion of employers doesn't check references.

Interviews

You must look like the employer's image of someone who can do the job successfully. Try to dress similarly to those currently holding the job or to the decision maker. As a general rule, if you are uncertain, business dress tends toward conservative styles and suits with skirts — but not pants. Molloy (1977) will provide ideas but is considered overly conservative by those in middle to upper management, where more individual freedom is allowed . . . and better discretion is expected. Don't be shy, but don't take over the interview. Most hiring decisions are made during the first few minutes of an interview, and the odds favor those with whom the interviewer is comfortable — especially if the interviewer feels free to do most of the talking. When you have the opportunity to ask questions, be prepared with incisive questions about the organization, policy, and the job that show your knowledge. Avoid asking questions concerning pay and benefits until the job looks won, and avoid academic jargon. Finally, interviewers feel most certain of those who are like themselves—if you are similar, emphasize it; if not, deemphasize it. Similarities include management style and ideas, sex, college background, class, religion, nationality, hometown, and politics (cf. Larwood & Blackmore, 1978; Schneier, 1977). Don't be upset if you don't get the first jobs you interview for; research indicates that interviewers have little—often worse than chance—ability to make appropriate decisions (Mayfield, 1964; Turnage & Muchinsky, 1984; Ulrich & Trumbo, 1965).

What to Present

If you still have the choice, try to do your thesis or dissertation on some topic with a recognized application. You don't have to abandon theory to do this, but you should be comfortable explaining how your theory can be applied, why business should apply it, and how your working for a business doing or applying this type of research is beneficial to the business. Don't be shy.

No one wants a long list of courses, but there are some other items on your resume, in your interview, or in your cover letter that will be helpful. Be brief in all cases except when you are so certain of your target that your presentation will overwhelm and astound. Read a short business text and the company annual reports if available. Just like the *Chronicle of Higher Education*, every business sector and every field has its relevant journals. If your interests are sufficiently focused, subscribe to the trade journals (e.g., *Ad Week, Wall Street Journal, Chain Store Age, Canadian Petroleum*) in your area of interest. These will catch you up on the techniques and jargon important to you. Write a brief paragraph for your cover letter or, if room permits, your resume, using industry jargon (assuming you really understand it), describing how your background uniquely qualifies you to work on the type of projects you are applying for. Make the paragraph appealing, but avoid pleas, condescension, or jargon foreign to the industry. Prepare to bring up your training and defend it in your interview.

Experience

Background and experience are frequently needed. You can easily get these. Try the following: target your dissertation (see above), do private consulting with local firms, comparatively test any firm's ads with college students, publish some relevant research articles, analyze the industry comparatively and show how the target firm comes out relative to competitors, show the cost effectiveness of the new activity for which you are recommending yourself. There is a point regarding experience that most of us tend to forget when we are facing a potential employer in the moment of truth: you already have all of the experience you will ever need. . . the rest is just specialized training in relating the experience to your job. Research indicates that about half of interviewees lie concerning important questions and inflate their past background in a seemingly desirable direction (cf. Anderson, Warner, & Spencer, 1984). Since you are competing with these people, make certain that you place your own abilities and background in the best possible light (also remember that lying is grounds for dismissal if you are caught). A woman in Los Angeles made the transition to management by relating the following when she was asked how her academic background had prepared her for the teamwork and conflict management required by management: "if you had grown up in a family with one potato for dinner and two hungry brothers, you wouldn't need to ask."

Something Special

Differentiate yourself from the rest of the applicants by doing something different — if you can and if it makes sense. A friend of mine decided to quit college just prior to completing her Ph.D. in Literature. She obtained a mailing list of firms with internal advertising agencies from the library at the Chamber of Commerce and began a direct mail advertising campaign to them. Every three weeks, she sent them a card identified with a sketch of a chess knight and the words "Paladin Copywriter — have pen, will travel" followed by a clever paragraph explaining her assets and her phone number. Before the third mailing, she had three job offers and is now (three years later) earning over twice what a junior professor would be paid. As a postscript, she has also won a national fiction award for published work that she hadn't time to do while teaching and writing her dissertation. Since business is conservative, any gimmicks such as this should be appropriate to the job being sought; otherwise they may waste your opportunities.

Getting in the Door

Most positions are never advertised (Parnes, 1970). They are obtained through friends via word of mouth. This suggests that you should let the widest possible number of people know of your availability and qualifications. Mine your contacts thoroughly, by asking them for their contacts, for example. You should also join networks in your target fields. It may take a while, but every locale and every type of activity has its networks and these function as active clearing houses for job information and contacts. Ask your friends what the comparable groups are to Association for Women in Computing, American Association of Personnel Women, Women in Business, Women in Management (addresses of some relevant organizations are listed in the Appendixes). Large firms, such as AT&T and TRW, have internal women's networks which function in the same way. If your friends can't help you, understand that you will be better advised to mount a mail and telephone campaign than to wait for an advertised opening (but try that too). The advertised jobs already have been picked over by someone else's friends and have a maximum number of competitors who may have a more traditional background. For your campaign, get a list of firms from any of the following: Chamber of Commerce lists of industrial firms by area, trade association lists of members engaged in a particular activity, membership lists of professionals in this field, circulation lists of trade journals, professional mailing list houses, Yellow Pages lists of those in trade or commerce, or the local library if you are in one of the largest cities. (See also Gore's and Shepela's chapters for further suggestions.)

Don't count them out, but the following are less productive: newspaper ads (unless in a selective trade journal) — especially blind box ads; recruiters (unless you use them to determine whom to contact yourself), and placement services.

When you have sent something to a firm, follow up with a phone call within 10 days. Ask that person if you have contacted the appropriate individual, and determine whether he or she knows of a more appropriate contact within the firm — or at another organization. Use this contact as a personal referral on your second contact if possible. Ask whether it is all right to call back in a few weeks. Above all, make each contact lead to another. The jobs are there, but you have to find them.

Discrimination

Sex and race discrimination still exist in industry — often to a somewhat larger extent than in academic life (cf. Blau & Ferber, 1985). Thus Black and white women are paid less, are given fewer opportunities for promotion, are promoted into less important areas of organizations, and are less likely to be hired for meaningful (challenging and important) positions in the first place (Larwood & Gutek, 1984). Don't let that fool you, however. The prize is worth the aggravation. Statistics indicate that the higher your level in the organization and the higher your level of education, the less discrimination you will experience relative to majority males. Nonetheless, you can cut the likelihood and amount of discrimination you will experience in the following ways: get the support of important people in and outside of the organization, be certain that you publicize your achievements within the organization, objectify your achievements so that they cannot be discounted, work for organizations which make a fetish of equal employment opportunity and which can point to a successful history of promoting and helping women and minorities, and join and work with women's networks. Since no one likes to be threatened, don't expect a lot of mileage out of threatening to sue . . . and never sue unless you are ready to retire or change careers. For further information on discrimination and both tactics and options to combat it, you may find the following references helpful: Fenn (1980), Harragan (1977), Josefowitz (1980), Larwood, Gutek, and Gattiker (1984), Larwood and Wood (1977), Nieva and Gutek (1981), and Stromberg and Harkess (in press). If your interest is purely academic, the two leading sources are a journal, *Sex Roles*, and a new annual volume, *Women and Work: An Annual Review*.

DEALING WITH TWO FRIGHTENING MYTHS

There are two myths that, if true, would be scary indeed. The first is the myth that job security is close to nonexistent in business. Many academics see this as a rationale for accepting lower pay and often significantly worse working conditions in academia. It is certainly true that large numbers are fired in industry, and that it can happen with little warning. It is also true, however, that most would-be academics fail to achieve tenure (many never find academic jobs despite considerable effort), and that many are stuck in what students recognize as dead-end jobs. The effect of tenure is to carve a sharp division between the haves and the have nots. With no such thing as tenure, industry provides an easier entry and a better opportunity for recovery by those who are let go than does academia. Those who are truly good need not fear loss of their job . . . and have multiple opportunities if that should occur.

A second myth (perpetuated by industry for obvious reasons) is that one works one's way from the bottom (sweeping the floor) to the top (commanding from the penthouse). Rosenbaum (1985, p. 124) found that most management jobs studied over a period from 1962 to 1975 were either abolished or newly created in the period; "Persistence is more the exception than the rule." In other words, the existence of chains of progression from the bottom to the top is illusory; actual career progressions do not have the chance to move along them. From a practical standpoint, this means that you can convince management to create a new job for you at some place in the middle. If you are perceived as a person worth having, the nonexistence of a job will not prevent your being hired. Similarly, no one lives long enough to move from the bottom of General Motors to the top; the skills needed at the bottom are different from those required at the top in any event. Don't be fooled into thinking you need to start at the entry level; begin where you feel comfortable.

CONCLUSION

Two-thirds of the students whose dissertation committees I have chaired have turned their backs on teaching. All of these individuals were sufficiently good to obtain fine academic jobs if they had wanted them. In fact, they felt that industry offered higher pay, more interesting work, and less consuming involvement. The careers they entered are varied, including individual management consulting, working for consulting firms, personnel training, career development in a personnel department, and marketing research. Rather than filling up, the opportunities for others looking for these positions are increasing as the pioneers show what those with scholarly training can do. We have the research skills, the interests, and usually the background needed to succeed in business. I have no doubt that the future will see larger numbers of us moving in this direction.

REFERENCES

Anderson, C. D., Warner, J. L., & Spencer, C. C. (1984). Inflation bias in self-assessment examinations: Implications for valid employee selection. *Journal of Applied Psychology, 69,* 574–580.

Blau, F. D., & Ferber, M. A. (1985). Women in the labor market: The last twenty years. In L. Larwood, A. H. Stromberg, & B. A. Gutek (Eds.), *Women and work: An annual review* (Vol. 1). Beverly Hills: Sage.

Bolster, B. I., & Springbett, B. M. (1961). The reaction of interviewers to favorable and unfavorable information. *Journal of Applied Psychology, 45,* 97–103.

Fenn, M. (1980). *In the spotlight: Women executives in a changing environment.* Englewood Cliffs, NJ: Prentice-Hall.

Harragan, B. L. (1977). *Games mother never taught you.* New York: Rawson.

Josefowitz, N. (1980). *Paths to power: A woman's guide from first job to top executive.* Reading, MA: Addison-Wesley.

Larwood, L., & Blackmore, J. (1978). Sex discrimination in managerial selection: testing predictions of the vertical dyad linkage model. *Sex Roles, 4,* 359–367.

Larwood, L., & Gutek, B. (1984). Women at work in the United States. In M. J. Davidson & C. L. Cooper (Eds.), *Working women: An international survey.* Chichester, U.K.: John Wiley.

Larwood, L., Gutek, B. A., & Gattiker, U. E. (1984). A model of institutional discrimination and resistance to change. *Group and Organization Studies, 9,* 333–352.

Larwood, L., & Wood, M. M. (1977). *Women in management.* Boston, MA: Lexington Books.

Mayfield, E. C. (1964). The selection interview: A reevaluation of published research. *Personnel Psychology, 17,* 239–260.

Molloy, J. T. (1977). *The woman's dress for success book.* New York: Warner Books.

Nieva, V. F., & Gutek, B. A. (1981). *Women and work: A psychological perspective.* New York: Praeger.

Parnes, H. S. (1970). Labor force and labor markets. In *A review of industrial relations research* (Vol. 1). Madison: University of Wisconsin, Industrial Relations Association.

Rosenbaum, J. E. (1985). Persistence and change in pay inequalities: Implications for job evaluation and comparable worth. In L. Larwood, A. H. Stromberg, & B. A. Gutek (Eds.), *Women and work: An annual review* (Vol. 1). Beverly Hills: Sage.

Schneier, C. E. (1977). The influence of raters' cognitive characteristics on the reliability and validity of rating scales. *Academy of Management Proceedings*, 255–259.

Shaffer, D. R., & Tomarelli, M. (1981). Bias in the ivory tower: An unintended consequence of the Buckley amendment for graduate admissions? *Journal of Applied Psychology, 66,* 7–11.

Stromberg, A. H., & Harkess, S. (In press). *Women working: Theories and facts in perspective* (2nd ed.). Palo Alto, CA: Mayfield.

Turnage, J. J., & Muchinsky, P. M. (1984). A comparison of the predictive validity of assessment center evaluations versus traditional measures in forecasting supervisory job performance: Interpretive implications of criterion distortion for the assessment paradigm. *Journal of Applied Psychology, 69,* 595–602.

Ulrich, L., & Trumbo, D. (1965). The selection interview since 1949. *Psychological Bulletin, 63,* 100–116.

■ APPENDIXES

Checklist for
the First Academic Job Search

BEFORE THE JOB SEARCH YEAR

- Start reading job notices at least a year before you plan to apply.
- Get on a search committee for a faculty position as a graduate student member, if possible.
- Cultivate relationships with three to five people who can write letters of recommendation for you.
- Look at the vitae (academic resumes) of more advanced graduate students.
- Prepare your own vita and a three-to-five page research statement.

THE JOB SEARCH

- Keep a file of job ads.
- Keep a calendar of due dates for applications.
- When deciding how many jobs to apply for, include jobs you may not be sure of, but eliminate those you'd never consider accepting.
- Don't be hesitant about calling the institution to find out more about the job, but be prepared to make a good impression on the phone.
- Rehearse your colloquium to an audience of graduate students.
- Prepare other items for your talk (e.g., slides).

THE INTERVIEW

- Wear something you are comfortable in, but that looks serious.
- Be prepared to do lots of walking.
- Read the papers of the faculty at the place you're being interviewed, especially if they are close to your area.
- Prepare your own set of questions about the place.
- Talk to the graduate students there.
- Ask about 'seed' money for research, campus research funds available, research assistant arrangements, research space and equipment, and availability of work-study students.
- Ask about computer time and terminals.
- Find out about the availability of research leaves for untenured faculty.
- Find out what your teaching load will be and what other expectations there are for what you will be teaching (e.g., how often will you have to teach that introductory course?)
- Ask about salary. If you have had a postdoc, you may be able to negotiate a higher salary. Find out how salary raises are determined. For instance, is it based solely on number of publications per year? Is summer salary available?
- Try to find out what is emphasized in terms of getting tenure (research, teaching, service?).
- Inquire about grant issues. What help is there in terms of attracting outside funding? If you get a grant, what potential is there for buying time out of teaching?
- What kind of support services are there in terms of secretarial support, xeroxing, phone, work-study students?

LONG-RANGE PLANNING

- Finish your dissertation at least two to three months before starting your job.
- Develop good relationships with students and faculty at your graduate institution.
- Write to selected others in your research area about your research, starting in graduate school.
- Buy a lottery ticket.

Relevant Professional Organizations

Academy of Management. Contact: Walter Newson, P.O. Drawer K2, Mississippi State University, Mississippi State, MS 39762. The Academy has a *Women in Management* Division.

American Association for the Advancement of Science, 1333 H Street, N.W., Washington, DC 20005, (202)326-6670.

Office of Opportunities in Science, AAAS office, Shirley Malcom (Head). (Provides information concerning opportunities in science for women, minorities, and the physically disabled.)

American Association of Marriage and Family Counselors, 225 Yale Avenue, Claremont, California 91711.

American Association of University Women, 2401 Virginia Avenue N.W., Washington, DC 20037, (202)785-7700. (Distributes a *Job Hunters's Kit.*)

American Historical Association, 400 A Street S.E., Washington, DC 20003, (202)544-2422. (Distributes *A Survival Manual for Women (and Other) Historians.*)

Other women's history committees and groups:

American Historical Association Committee on Women Historians, Linda Levy Peck (Chair), Department of History, Purdue University, West Lafayette, IN 47907.

Association of Black Women Historians, Rosalyn Terborg-Penn (Co-director), 5484 Sleeping Dog Lane, Columbia, MD 21045, and Sharon Harley (Co-director), Afro-American Studies Department, University of Maryland, College Park, MD 20742.

American Psychiatric Association, 1400 K Street N.W., Washington, DC 20005, (202)682-6000.

American Psychological Association, 1200 17th Street N.W., Washington, DC 20036, (202)955-7600.

Committees, divisions, and sections affiliated with APA:

Committee on Lesbian and Gay Concerns, APA office. (Among other functions, distributes a roster of lesbian and gay therapists.)

Committee on Women in Psychology, Ursula Delworth (Chair), APA office.
Division 35 *(Psychology of Women)*, Julia Ramos-McKay (Secretary-Treasurer), 120 Esquire Drive, Manchester, CT 06040.
Division 35 *Section on Black Women*, Gwen Puryear Keita (Membership chair), University Counseling Service, Howard University, Washington, DC 20059.
Division 44 *(Gay and Lesbian Psychologists)*, Allan Pinka (Secretary), 3210 Dewitt Drive, Los Angeles, CA 90068.
Women's Programs, APA office, Renee Garfinkel (Administrative Officer). (Distributes directories of Black and Hispanic women in psychology and of psychotherapy resources for women.)
American Society for Training and Development, 1630 Duke Street, Alexandria, VA 22313, (703)683-8100.
American Sociological Association, 1722 N Street N.W., Washington, DC 20036, (202)833-3410.
Association of Lesbian and Gay Psychologists, 210 Fifth Avenue, New York, New York 10010.
Association for Women in Psychology, K. Towns & Rie Gentzler (Membership co-chairs), Crags-PSU/Capitol Campus, Middletown, PA 17057.
Association for Women in Science, 2401 Virginia Avenue, Suite 303, Washington, DC 20037, (202)833-1998. Diane Tycer, Executive Director.
Association for Women in Social Work, P.O. Box 110, Dowelltown, TN 37059.
Association for Women in Sociology, Janet Chafetz (President), Department of Sociology, University of Houston, Houston, TX 77004.
Modern Language Association, 10 Aster Place, New York, NY 10003, (212) 475-9500.
Committees and divisions affiliated with MLA:
Commission on the Status of Women in the Profession and *Division on Women's Studies in Language and Literature*, MLA office.
National Association of Social Workers, 7981 Eastern Avenue, Silver Spring, MD 20910, (301)565-0333.
National Women's Studies Association, University of Maryland, College Park, MD 20742, (301)454-3757.
NWSA *Lesbian Caucus*, Pat Gozemba (Coordinator), English Department, Salem State, Salem, MA 01970.
NWSA *Women of Color Caucus*, Benita Hampton (Coordinator), Women's Studies Program, SUNY-Buffalo, 1010 Clemins Hall, Buffalo, NY 14261.
Project on the Status and Education of Women, Association of American Colleges, 1818 R Street N.W., Washington, DC 20009.
Society for Women in Philosophy, Marilyn Friedman (Newsletter editor), Department of Philosophy, Bowling Green University, Bowling Green, OH 43403.

Additional Useful References[1]

Abel, E. K. (1984). *Terminal degrees: The job crisis in higher education.* New York: Praeger.

DeSole, G., & Hoffmann, L. (Eds.). (1981). *Rocking the boat: Academic women and academic processes.* New York: Modern Language Association.

Farley, J. (1981). *Academic women and employment discrimination: A critical annotated bibliography.* Ithaca, NY: ILR Publications.

Hall, R.M., & Sandler, B.R. (1983). *Academic mentoring for women students and faculty: A new look at an old way to get ahead.* Washington, DC: Association of American Colleges, Project on the Status and Equality of Women. (Address listed in appendix of relevant professional organizations.)

Kaufman, H.G. (1982). *Professionals in search of work: Coping with the stress of job loss and unemployment.* New York: Wiley.

Linehan, M. M. (1983). Interviewing to get the job. *Behavior Therapist, 6*, 3-4.

Mullins, C.J. (1977). *A guide to writing and publishing in the social and behavioral sciences.* New York: Wiley.

Risser, N.A., & Wyman, R.E. (1984). *Humanities Ph.D.s and nonacademic careers.* Evanston, IL: Committee on Institutional Cooperation. (990 Grove Street, Evanston, IL 60201.)

Spencer, M.L., Kehow, M., & Speece, K. (Eds.) (1982). *Handbook for women scholars: Strategies for success.* San Francisco: Behavioral Research Corporation, Center for Women Scholars.

[1]Thanks is extended to Jacqueline Macaulay and Eleanor Hall for providing a number of these references.

Theodore, A. (1986). *The campus troublemakers: Academic women in protest.* Houston: Cap & Gown Press.

Thompson, I., & Roberts, A. (Eds.). (1985). *The road retaken: Women reenter the academy.* New York: Modern Language Association.

Tolpin, M. (1981). *A woman's guide to academe: Moving in, moving, moving over.* Wellesley, MA: Higher Education Resource Service.

Udolf, R. (1976). *The college instructor's guide.* Chicago: Nelson Hall.

Index